ENTREPRENEURSHIP

A WEALTH-CREATION AND VALUE-ADDING PROCESS

RAYMOND W.Y. KAO

University of Toronto, Canada
Nanyang Technological University, Singapore

PRENTICE HALL

New York   London   Toronto   Sydney   Tokyo   Singapore

First published 1995 by
Prentice Hall
Simon & Schuster (Asia) Pte Ltd
Alexandra Distripark
Block 4, #04-31
Pasir Panjang Road
Singapore 0511

Cover photograph by Weinberg/Clark and The Image Bank

Printed in Singapore

1 2 3 4 5   99 98 97 96 95

ISBN 0-13-324765-1

Prentice Hall International (UK) Limited, *London*
Prentice Hall of Australia Pty. Limited, *Sydney*
Prentice Hall Canada Inc., *Toronto*
Prentice Hall Hispanoamericana, S.A., *Mexico*
Prentice Hall of India Private Limited, *New Delhi*
Prentice Hall of Japan, Inc., *Tokyo*
Editora Prentice Hall do Brasil, Ltda., *Rio de Janeiro*
Prentice Hall, Inc., *Englewood Cliffs, New Jersey*

ENTREPRENEURSHIP

A WEALTH-CREATION AND VALUE-ADDING PROCESS

Contents

Foreword

Entrepreneurship has been lauded by many as the essential ingredient for the economic well-being of a nation. It has been championed for its job-creating capability: it transfers people from the category of "the unemployed" to that of "the self-employed" and the entrepreneurs through their ventures provide employment to others. This job-creating capability of entrepreneurship is not the sole reason for encouraging entrepreneurship. The enterprises developed by entrepreneurs do contribute to the economy — but is that all there is to entrepreneurship? Is it confined to those in the business sector? What is there to prevent it from applying to and pervading the rest of society? What is wrong with the form of entrepreneurship as it is understood today (limited to the business realm)? More importantly, what are the underpinning assumptions we have about the polity, the economy, the corporation, and the role of the individual in each of the foregoing entities that restrict entrepreneurship? These are some of the questions that Raymond poses in this book.

As you read this book you might discover, as I have, your discomfort growing as what you have assumed to be the way things should be, are being called into question. Who would have thought that classical economics, the theory of the firm, and the corporate and securities regulations — fundamental to the understanding and fabric of modern corporate life — threaten the "life" of their very offspring, the firm, by "dehumanizing" it and rendering it "entrepreneurless". The economists and the accountants are taken to task for dehumanizing the firm. Whither the "spirit of entrepreneurship" in the firm? Not only does he question our acceptance of the separation between ownership and management in the corporation (sacrosanct in America from the days of Berle and Means), he asks difficult questions about what many would consider to be "motherhood and apple pie": democracy, capitalism and the free market economy.

What a cynic, you might think. One might be justified in thinking thus if one did not read on till the end of the book because he appears to be irreverent not only about economics, but also about management science for which he has scathing remarks. Even religion has not escaped his attention: the motivational impetus of religion is discussed in relation to his perception of what the key to it all is: motivation (Chapter 6).

In truth, all he actually does is "call a spade a spade". He has been consistent in not leaving any stone unturned in his effort to get the reader to re-examine precepts. He has done so in a not too conventional manner. In the same unconventional manner, he has done me the great honour of asking me to write the foreword for his book: a book which I feel is his crowning work in the field of entrepreneurship as it embodies his convictions. He has written two other highly regarded texts on entrepreneurship and small business management with this book differing from the earlier ones in that it is not just a "how to" book. It is a special distinction for me since Raymond did not follow the convention of inviting a notable personality, better still, a luminary to write the foreword. Instead he asked me. It is a rare honour since I am relatively unknown and consider myself to be a learner in this field, and having learnt much from him from the privilege of co-teaching Entrepreneurship and Enterprising Development with him in the past year. Raymond, on the other hand, has earned various distinctions including that of Distinguished Professor of Entrepreneurship. Yet if you know Raymond, you will appreciate that this is consistent with his character. To provide a little insight, let me share one of his unconventional practices. On birthdays, as expected, a celebration is accompanied by the presentation of presents to the birthday person. On the contrary, in the Kao household, on his children's birthdays, Raymond has his children give presents to their mother.

Central to his thesis are the definitions of entrepreneurship, the entrepreneurship and enterprising culture in Chapter 5. He contends that for the individual, the corporation and the economy, entrepreneurship cannot be defined as the pursuit of profit (Chapter 3) or justified only for the rate of return on investment (Chapter 4). It is through these definitions and a willingness to re-examine and break free from our mindsets and theoretical underpinnings that entrepreneurship will lead to change, innovation and empowerment for the individual, the corporation and the society. Entrepreneurship is a matter of attitude with attitudes being redirected by the new definitions. It is a mindset that is independent of the political and economic environment (Chapter 1).

You will find this book replete with examples from Raymond's personal life, from other writers and from history. It is these personal stories, and observations that endear his arguments and vision to the reader.

"To know the disease is half the cure", so the proverb goes, so one might see value in what Raymond has to say without reading the whole book since he has identified the ills and that is half the job. However, he is not content with identifying definitions or merely highlighting the ills. He is not a theorist but a pragmatist and provides not "a highway to heaven" but pointers for the "road to economic freedom" for a meaningful existence as an individual or an employee (obviously the meaning will stem from being engaged in a wealth and value creating process). He gives an elaborate illustration of how a corporation may through the issuance of "stakes" to its employees motivate them through "ownership" to passion and his form of entrepreneurship (Chapter 9).

With more of Kao's type of entrepreneur, the world would be a better place since profit, that illusory concept whose various definitions Raymond explores, is not all that makes for value.

Wee-Liang Tan
Singapore

Preface

"Entrepreneurship" has become the catchword of our time. To support entrepreneurship these days is to support motherhood. Politicians herald it as a fountain of employment, the generator of new jobs for our new generations. Idealists (if you prefer, dreamers) pose entrepreneurship as the solution to the problems of two diametrically opposed ideologies: socialism on the one hand, and capitalism on the other. To business persons, it is a new coat of paint on their old practices; instead of the old accusations of profiteering and exploitation, they are now hailed as the saviours of the free enterprise system and the market economy. Even the academics like it: it is the new kid on the academic block, to be studied and explored, and fitted into the existing patterns of academic research with countless new studies and publications. I suppose that I fall into this category myself. After all, I find that there is something exciting about teaching entrepreneurship, even though many complain that entrepreneurship is something that cannot be taught.

Unfortunately, most of the hype about entrepreneurship turns out to be little more than just words, because as a group, we have little sense of what entrepreneurship really is. For the most part, we believe that entrepreneurship is about owning a business and making money. Some people are misled by the success stories of the few and advertisements for "get rich quick" schemes (some even think that entrepreneurship will provide them with a highway to heaven). Entrepreneurship is both more or less than these misconceptions. It is no highway to heaven and it will never make you rich enough to buy a person's loyalty or love, but it is certainly more than just a matter of making a profit: it is a vehicle with which to achieve at least one type of freedom, economic freedom, without which there is no freedom at all.

Unfortunately, entrepreneurship has been used harmfully, and in the name of entrepreneurship and ultimately profit, various criminals and profiteers have done much damage to our individual rights and freedom, to our health and to the health of our environment and our planet.

Although this book is not intended to reshape the world, every opportunity to expose the reader to some fundamental questions about civilizations, our culture and our environment has been taken. It is hoped that by posing these questions and attempting to provide some answers to them, the individual will be encouraged to create rather than just use, and, under the auspices of entrepreneurial culture, add value to society. Through our collective wisdom, we can build a society which is environmentally and socially conscious, and which will stand our children and grandchildren in good stead, long after we ourselves are gone.

Writing this book has been a moving experience for me. Describing some of my past ordeals as a "third class refugee" during the Japanese invasion of China was almost like reliving them. When developing the graphic expression for a global picture of our life support system, I spent long nights struggling over the concepts of profit and rate of return on investment. I thought: "How can I be so naive and stupid as to go against profit and rate of return on investment? It is so fundamental to the way business operates; our world comes to a standstill without it." Then I recalled one story which illustrates my definition of entrepreneurship and made me realize how it applies to the real world (the sealed beam lamp example in this book). Entrepreneurship, I realized, is about making decisions, usually at personal risk. At its best, entrepreneurship is about making decisions when the personal risk is not part of the decision making process: you do what you have to do, because it must be done. In this context, entrepreneurship is really about considering the needs of the many before the needs of one. Ultimately, of course, we must do things for ourselves or we will not survive. It is a question of how we do it. I am reminded of an old saying: If I give a man a fish, then I feed him for a day. If I teach a man to fish, then I feed him for life. But if I teach a man to fish responsibly, then not only do I feed him but the rest of his village as well, for generations to come. It is only in the last case that a profit is really made, because there can be no profit if our environment is harmed.

This book contains a large number of thoughts, some of which are my own and are presented as stories. Some others, which may have been said or written by many people at different times (maybe even thousands of years ago) in different parts of the world, are difficult, if not impossible, to trace their origins. However, where sources are known, credit has been given. On the other hand, I must express my gratitude and offer my apologies to those thinkers whose names I was unable to find and the sources of publication I was unable to track down.

In writing this book I am indebted to many people. If my gratitude means anything to those who helped me complete this book, then I must say that my gratitude exceeds my ability to express it. At any rate, I wish to thank my wife Flora and our son Rowland, both of whom helped me with this manuscript and gave me the strength to finish it.

I take full reponsibility for this book. In case there is anything offensive or inappropriate, then the guilt is all mine. I guess that if someone dislikes it enough, then he can always send me a one-way ticket to heaven. As an entrepreneur, I consider it an opportunity, and I am grateful for that as well.

As my gratification, I dedicate this book to the entrepreneurs the world over who have a concern for the environment, create wealth for themselves and add value to the society, and I congratulate the people of Singapore who have created a thrilling nation which would have caught Adam Smith by surprise.

"He", "him" or "his", when used in a general sense in this book, refers to both genders.

1

The Greatest Balancing Act on Earth: To Link Democracy, Market Economy and Entrepreneurship

Equally important, the postwar system in most liberal democratic capitalist countries gave capital a decisive upper hand in dictating the pattern of organizational innovation and structure change. The result has been an economic and political standoff in which business elite and the citizenry alike have veto power over economic change but share a nonviable common vision of economic future (Bowles and Gintis, 1986: 6).

Democracy

"Democracy" is a shining word portrayed by our politicians as the political system for the whole world. As a retired politician (not an American, by the way) once said:

Now we have the democratic system working for all the people in the world. People in some parts of the world never had a government of their own

1

choice, but were put together by some king, queen or forced by a group of individuals not representing their wish. Nowadays, the people have found a way to band together as a country, a country governed by a government who is there elected by the people, of the people and for the people.

In addition to democracy, there are two other words, "market economy" and "entrepreneurship", two words so fashionable that politicians more often than not link them together, defining a particular brand of democracy. It is a democracy with a market economy in an environment stimulating, nurturing and developing entrepreneurship, thus making this society so prosperous that everyone can enjoy human rights including freedom from poverty (in the author's interpretation, a human right) and peace on earth. To understand this relationship to entrepreneurship and how it works in the democratic and market economy environment as portrayed by western leaders, the topic of democracy as it relates to the market economy and entrepreneurship will be examined as an introduction to this book's deliberation.

The Origins of Ancient Democracy

Ancient democracy, on record, originated in the first half of the fifth century BC, a transformation that took place in political ideals and institutions of the Greek city state of Athens and those who emulated her. The concept worked because the population was small and it was possible for everyone to be involved in the government. Decisions were made by small assemblies and everyone had an opportunity and responsibility to hold public office (Dahl, 1915: 13–14). With the increase in the size of the "demos" (i.e. the people) it became necessary to modify the orginal concept. This modification led to modern democratic ideas and institutions that have been shaped by many other factors, of which three are particularly important: a republican tradition, the development of representative governments, and certain conclusions that tend to follow from a belief in political equality.

While republicanism was more than a simple reaffirmation of the ideals and practices of Greek democracy, a further development led the republicans to the task of designing a constitution reflecting and balancing the interests of the one, the few, or the many by providing for a mixed government of democracy, aristocracy, and monarchy so constituted that all three components would finally concur for the good of all. In the eighteenth century, the United States developed a strain of radical republicanism that in some respects reflected the older tradition.

Majority Rule

As life evolved, nations throughout the world, in time and need, have developed their own style of governing, but it is commonly accepted that if a democratic system is to be meaningful to the mass populace, the majority rule that amplifies collective decision making appears to be what it needs for the practice of democracy to be effective. Of course, there have been many questions concerning majority rule, such as the exclusive use of the majority principle. While people support democracy, what rule do they actually adopt in practice? Some form of majority rule is pretty much the standard solution despite its interpretations or how it is perceived by different people. Nevertheless, until this day, there seems to be no satisfactory answers to the above question. Despite this, people who support majority rule claim:

- It maximizes self-determination.
- It is a necessary consequence of reasonable requirement.
- It is more likely to produce correct decisions.
- It maximizes utility.

While there have been many criticisms of these justifications, the majority rule idea seems to stay with the democratic process worldwide. Yet there are questions with no satisfactory answers. What must be done is to have an open-minded attitude to accommodate practical implications experienced in different parts of the world in their attempt to practise the process of democracy.

Countries are Different, So are People and Their Interpretations and Practices of Democracy

A philosopher commenting about life itself, said that "life is just like driving wagons on the road; even though we travel the same road, we never travel on the same track." It is much the same with countries that practise democracy. There are different brands of democracy, and it is very much like running a household: everybody runs a household, but each household is run differently. Firstly, let us look at Hong Kong.

Hong Kong, as we all know, has been a British colony since the late nineteenth century. Hong Kong is to be returned to China because over 90 per cent of the colony (Kowloon) was leased from China for a period of ninety-nine years and without Kowloon, Hong Kong cannot survive. It is now a few years before Britain returns the colony to China, and the governor of Hong Kong wants to negotiate with the Chinese government for "more democracy" for Hong Kong. The governor must be congratulated for his efforts to bring out the reality that Hong Kong, after being governed by Britain for such a long time, has no real democracy. It is no wonder the colony, which is about double the size of Singapore, and with a population at any time of no less than 4 million (now, possibly 6 to 7 million people including illegal immigrants) for approximately 120 years, has only one university to accommodate the needs of its people. Why a second university was not allowed in the colony for such a long time is anyone's guess (the Chinese University of Hong Kong was founded in 1963). Moreover, anyone living in Hong Kong would have experienced the harsh reality of high education costs for his children. There are insufficient educational institutions and parents have to endure extremely harsh financial burdens so their children can receive primary and secondary education in the colony. For more than 100 years, major posts in the Hong Kong government, particularly senior officers in the police department, have been held by the British. Moreover, when the British government decided to let their British subjects (citizens of Hong Kong are legally British subjects) have a way out of Hong Kong should they decide not to stay in Hong Kong once the colony was returned to China, they handpicked a certain number of "selected individuals" (a small fraction) to qualify for emigration to the UK. These decisions, depriving or limiting a citizen's right to education, particularly university education (of course, if you have money, you can go to England), and the selection of a privileged group as being more British than the others, are certainly not majority decisions. One cannot imagine that those majority decisions were made by the Hong Kong legislative assembly or more specifically, the governor who is the representative of the Crown that governs the colony. Who then is responsible? This is certainly not the same democratic process as witnessed in western countries, including Britain itself.

It is even more interesting, that after more than 140 years of colonial status, the people in Hong Kong have not yet learned how to be democratic. If they did learn, why was it necessary for only the governor to represent the whole island in negotiations with China for more democracy for Hong Kong? It is almost like a father taking his 140-year-old child by the hand to go to school and talk to the school principal about conditions for entrance. If this is democracy, how do we differentiate between imperialism and democracy?

Back in the United Kingdom, a form of democracy has been evolving steadily for at least 700 years. Its parliamentary system has been a model for many other nations, including Canada, Australia, India and Singapore. They have all benefited from the British way of government, and even the American system, though a little different, has maintained a spirit which nevertheless reflects its origin.

The difference with British democracy and the US version is that in Britain, the queen or king remains the head of state with no executive power in practice, despite plenty of it in theory. For example, in Canada, one of the two legislative bodies, the Senate, is appointed with appproval required from the head of state, the Queen. The Canadian Prime Minister badly wanted to appoint extra senators to facilitate the passage of the free trade agreement with the US, thus in a sense, the Queen had a chance to affect legislation in Canada by acting or not acting according to the Prime Minister's recommendation. Even though the majority of citizens of Canada did not perceive this piece of legislation to be for the common good, the free trade agreement was passed by the Senate with the additional senators appointed by the government. The people of Canada, however, exercised their rights to choose who should govern, and virtually wiped out the governing party from parliament in its 1993 election. The democratic process was thus eventually expressed, but in a way unfamiliar to, for example, Canada's democratic American neighbours.

If a democratic government depends on the virtue of its citizens, and its virtue consists of their dedication to the public good (rather than one's own interests or those of some particular part of the public), then the process of democracy at the least is to free its people from poverty. If one were to travel extensively through the US, one may wonder: what is going on? Here is a country that made so much sacrifice to help other countries to be democratic including sacrificing the lives of young Americans, rendering immeasurable financial support to other nations in need, and being a strong pillar behind every world organization, yet it is unable to free the masses of its people from poverty. Much criticism has also been raised in this respect. It has been said the American version of democracy is essentially engineered and backed by powerful, financially well-to-do individuals and groups. Whether it is for the common good is yet to be seen. Although the US Government is doing what it can to respond to the challenge, the nationwide medi-care scheme and massive efforts devoted to job creation for the less fortunate Americans are cases in point.

Canada's democracy has a parliamentary system very much the same as those in Britain, Singapore and Australia. Its democratic system places a great deal of emphasis on the common good, or more specifically, universality and equality for all. A Canadian can stand on any part of the Canadian soil, from St. John, Newfoundland to Vancouver, British Columbia, from Windsor, Ontario to Yellowknife in the Yukon and if the medical facilities are available, a traveller would receive the same medi-care as at home. On the other hand, the idea of equality for all has been, at times, carried too far, making the Canadian brand of democracy a hindrance to progress. The author recalled his personal experience while serving as a member of the Consultative Committee to a federal minister. It was at a press conference called by the minister to announce a certain government policy with respect to the development of entrepreneurship and to explain how such a policy may be implemented. The author was called by the minister, as a representative from the Consultative Committee, to join him to respond to questions from the media. When the minister announced that a national council would be created for the purpose of working on details for the implementation of the policy, a question was raised by a reporter on a matter of representation in the council. The author gave a brief response indicating that there would be fair representation from all ten provinces (this was the Consultative Committee's recommendation to the minister). People at the press conference immediately reacted to the structure of the council. They requested that the council must include special interest groups and identified the following:

- Various minority groups (with a fair representation of each visible minority group)
- Disabled groups
- Women's groups
- Native people
- Professionals
- Trade associations

In particular there must be a fair provincial representation based on language and the size of the population. Of course, the proposed council could not possibly accommodate all those requests (as an estimation, if all the requests were accommodated, the council would have a size of 1000 people or more). The final selection process was a difficult one, ending up with about twenty-five to thirty people on the council. The ideal of equality for all in the Canadian version of democracy can be clearly seen in this particular undertaking. The same has been experienced in other government undertakings as well.

Many politicians with a flare for universality must be convinced that there is no general path to democracy. The Costa Ricans have had their democracy without the aid of military forces (abolished in 1948–49), but for the Russians, without military intervention, one wonders at the potential fate of democracy. Japan on the other hand, where the military had become a powerful political actor in the 1930s, declared in its 1947 constitution (largely a creation of the United States military occupation) that it would never maintain land, sea and air forces. The provision was nevertheless watered down by the subsequent development of a national police reserve and then a national defence force, and now even some talk of considering its nuclear options. Its effect is to prevent military intervention within the political system.

In contrast to these other systems, China, whose government has remained the same since the completion of the Communist revolution in 1947, has opened its door to developing a market economy much the same as practised throughout the world, but with its political system intact. If changes are necessary, they will occur because of the needs of China, and not because of criticisms from others, be they government leaders, media or any other group of individuals (as reported by the Singapore Broadcasting Corporation on 21 November 1993). Of course, it might be said that the changes in China reflect the wishes of its people to the same extent which is to say, decisions will be made when and where necessary by the decision makers.

Under the circumstances, the only thing that can be said to our world politicians is that we must first recognize that people are different, democratic processes are different, hence we should accept and appreciate the differences. We may even benefit from the differences. Moreover, you may ask any political scientist whether absolute democracy exists in this real world of ours. If there ever was one, we would have to go back to ancient Greece where every citizen in the city-state of Athens was involved in government and decisions were made in small assemblies and groups; but we know very well that with the size of the nations of today, this is virtually impossible.

Market Economy

Market economy is like putting fish in a pond; the degree of freedom of the fish is conditioned by the size of the pond and the number of fish in the pond. In the world we live in today, we have a controlled market economy, regulated market economy, planned market economy, no matter how you put it, a market economy, but never a free market economy.

While democracy is the political Mecca of this era, in the mind and soul of "democratized individuals", the market economy is the beacon of human progress. What is amazing to the masses is that there has always been a market economy in every part of the world; not only in ancient Greece, China and Egypt, but also among African tribes, bands of Indians and in both peace and war. No one can deny that during World War II, until Pearl Harbour, the market economy was nevertheless working as usual between the United States of America and Japan.

The market economy came with the need for exchange. So long as there are goods and services unable to be consumed completely, and there is a need for the surplus by others, trade will begin; when there is trade, there is a market. The market economy exists in any political system, but with differences largely dependent on the level of government intervention. The relationship between the market economy and the government is like that between fish and the pond which they swim in, with the degree of freedom of the fish conditioned by the size of the pond and the number of fish in the pond. In the world today, we have controlled market economies, regulated market economies, and of course, planned market economies, they are all market economies, but never the free market economy.

Citizens and particularly business persons of any country have attitudes toward government intervention in their market economy which often depend less on their political beliefs than on the state of business. Those who are successful want as little government intervention as possible ("They say they've reformed taxes but mine keep on going up" or "What do you mean, I need a permit?"). Someone on the brink of being squeezed out of business by a huge corporation wants more regulation to stop ruthless mergers and takeovers. Someone whose firm has just encountered fierce competition of imports from a country with low costs calls for tighter import regulations, adjustment assistance, or both.

The author recalls an occasion when giving a public lecture in the Pacific Rim to a group of entrepreneurs (owners/managers). One individual asked the author a question concerning government intervention in the marketplace. In his question, he implied that in a market economy, a government should intervene as little as possible, since the market economy will determine its own equilibrium. The author did not respond to the question directly, but rather replied: "Assume that there is one bowl of rice that everyone in a large assembly would like to have, since they have been without food for days. Is it possible to have a market system under the circumstances?" The author's answer silenced the audience. After a few minutes of discussion, the audience realized that under the circumstances, a market economy would not work, and some form of intervention was necessary. Intervention is obviously a form of government.

The point of the matter is that a market economy cannot function, if there is nothing to market. Therefore, in order to have a market system function as we perceive, we must create goods (wealth) first. The market system can only work if there is a surplus.

Unfortunately, there is clear evidence that many of us do not understand or are unwilling to accept this simple truth in life. These include world leaders of some countries and academics who continue their efforts to push the virtue of the market economy as a universal panacea. This also includes the popular notion of encouraging socialist countries to transform to market economies without acknowledging the shortage of wealth in these countries.

Can we have a market economy, if there is nothing to market? How does a market economy work in some African nations and what can they market to EEC countries, NAFTA countries and ASEAN countries, to generate sufficient revenue to sustain their livelihood and economy? The answer is obvious. What is important is to realize that it is the entrepreneurial-driven economy that creates wealth, and the market economy is only one element of many forces that induce (or stimulate) creative or innovative entrepreneurial endeavours. There is a Canadian expression that the author would like to use on some of our politicians and academic friends: Can you get this into your fat head? There is no market economy if you do not have anything to market!

Governments intervene in the market economy differently in different countries. In some countries, there is a need for tighter control, other countries need stimulation, and many others simply require the government to act as a catalyst. Many governments (perhaps all governments) do all three. The most popular view held by people who claim they know all about the market economy, is that the government should create an environment that is favourable to capital investment and stimulates entrepreneurship. The following are a few essentials which are common to many countries:

1. Government should provide controls designed to protect the public interest and prevent market behaviour that may limit the scope of the market system. It also provides regulation in situations in which the market system contradicts the public interest (such as monopolies).

2. Government should act as a catalyst. The use of tax incentives to encourage the private sector to create venture capital pools is a case in point.

3. Government should provide stimulation to strategically important sectors where the market system, in the opinion of the government, fails to perform (direct or indirect government involvement of this nature). In general, government stimulation policies have one or more of four major goals:

   ○ To provide a favourable business climate, one that encourages business investment and encourages entrepreneurs to take risk. For example, deregulation is designed to facilitate venture formation and growth.
   ○ To facilitate the flow of funds to needy ventures. Government-guaranteed loan schemes in many countries is a case in point.
   ○ To give relief from administrative legislation and other paper-work burdens and simplify tax systems, for example.
   ○ To provide direct assistance, often through various incentive schemes.

Democracy, Free Enterprise and Market Economy

Some years ago, the Canadian Liberal Government was so concerned about the national interest that it introduced the Foreign Investment Review Act. This was designed essentially to provide some last minute attempts to prevent foreign takeovers of businesses which were vital to the interests of the Canadian economy. In particular, areas where corporate power concentration could be harmful to the national interest were targeted, such as the oil industry, banks and other resources-related businesses. The measure, in the opinion of large Canadian corporations, was an excessive government intervention. At least one large insurance company advertised in a national newspaper on a daily basis. The full page advertisement showed a bird (presumably, a Canadian goose) flying in the sky, with one line: "Free the enterprise". How effective that advertisement was I could not say, but the Liberal Party was defeated at the next election.

In western democracy, the government is not viewed as having a vital role in the marketplace, even in matters related to entrepreneur-managed small firms. For example, the well-known Bolton Committee report released in the early 1970s by the British government, suggested that a vital role for the government to play in the marketplace was to ensure that legislative bills passed through parliament do not have harmful effects on small businesses. The British government modified substantially its small business policies with programmes recognized worldwide, such as: the enterprise agency scheme and training and enterprise council programmes related to education, training and skills development. However, the real question to be answered is: is there such a thing as free enterprise in the market economy? The answer to this question is that market economy or not, there is no such thing as "free enterprise".

First of all, absolute freedom never exists in human institutions. If one person over-expresses his personal freedom, it will be an impediment to others' freedom. In the market economy, the system limits the enterprise's freedom. The barriers of entry, corporate power through advertising, cost advantage, research and development expenditures, mergers and acquisitions and, among other things, the channels of distribution, all limit the freedom of other enterprises. On the other hand, these can be considered as natural elements of competition. Competition always helps to improve performance, therefore, it is part of the package of the market economy, except where there is unfair competition, improper business conduct and above all public interest. On account of all this, it is fair to say that there is really no absolute freedom for an enterprise nor absolute freedom for any individual. Freedom is always conditioned by others' freedom. In the market economy, proper market behaviour is always the responsibility of the enterprises themselves (assume the enterprise is a firm, an entity), and it is the government's responsibility to ensure the enterprises behave properly in the marketplace. Democracy, free enterprise and market economy can be linked only in this fashion. Let us make it clear that we can always find democracy in political systems and governments, but we cannot find the same democracy in firms. Under the democratic system the government is supposed to be elected by the general populace for the common good of the people. Firms (corporations) are the mind and body of the market economy, and therefore, it is not a democratic place, no matter how much you may wish it. In corporations, "capital" talks, not the people. On the other hand, if corporations are powerful enough to influence government actions, then we really do not have democracy at all, except, the right to vote and veto.

Can We Link Democracy with the Market Economy?

The market economy exists under any and all political systems, but is not comparable with democracy for a number of reasons:

1. Market economy is capital driven, and since it is capital driven, it is capitalism, not democracy.

2. Whereas the firm is the actor in the market economy, and the firm under the theory of the firm is assumed to be an independent entity, the governance of the firm is by individuals not elected by members of the firm, but appointed by the equity holders of the firm who invested capital in the firm. Therefore, although in the democratic process, the government is governed by elected representatives, the firm in the market economy, is governed by the equity or capital holders.

3. The elected government in a democratic process is supposed to work for the common good, and the appointed managers of a firm work to achieve the firm's goal — profit. Since the firm is held by equity or capital holders, therefore, everyone in the firm under the appointed managers are supposed to be working for the shareholders' interests.

4. Democracy promotes the individual's rights, whereas the market economy under the theory of the firm promotes capital accumulation. Individuals' rights within the firm are dependent on the power of a trade union or at the discretion of the firm's management.

5. The voting process in democracy is one person one vote, unlike a firm's voting process, either at the shareholders' meeting or meeting

of the board of directors. Only those holding capital can vote, and it is not one person one vote, but one share one vote. The number of votes is based on the number of shares held, not based on the number of people at the meeting.

6. In the market economy under the theory of the firm it is capital that rules not the majority.

7. Individuals working in the firm have no right to participate in the governing of the firm, no right to vote decisions that are vital to the health of the firm, and the public and no right to veto any bad management decisions.

Under the circumstances, it is clear that the market economy is a capital-driven economy. It has brought many people wealth and a broad-based improvement of living standards depending on the level of technology, availability of resources and human contributions. But as capital drives a firm to better performance in order to satisfy the capital holders' desire for higher profit, the management of the firm must find more creative and innovative activities to improve the firm's performance. There may be a possibility of finding entrepreneurially driven individuals in the firm and using capital to engage in creative and innovative activities. However, the firm might not be able to improve its performance because the individuals in the firm do not share the same goal as the firm. The management must then find other means to improve performance. In meeting competitive pressures, sometimes at the cost of job loss, there will be downsizing, restructuring, plant relocation and the substitution of labour for technology, heavily taxing material resources, and finally taxing the environment. No wonder there are countless polluted lakes unfit to provide life support, acid rain and acid particles cast over the sky in industrial cities, and high levels of air contamination which more often than not have made large numbers of innocent residents suffer from health problems.

The capital-driven market economy may have done well in providing wealth to some individuals on a short term basis, but it really has very little to do with democracy, unless individuals in the firm are given the right to participate in management. Alternatively, they have the right to vote for the people chosen to manage the firm. Some politicians claim that democracy is the form of government which best supports a healthy market economy providing stable government, creating a better business climate and inducing capital investment. However, China, despite its Communist political system which differs greatly from the western democracies, is attracting capital investment that surpasses that of any other western nation, such as Canada, UK, France or Germany. On the other hand, Russia is at present practising western democracy, but has to rely on the G7 to pump billions of US dollars to support its government. How can it be possible to say that only certain democracies can attract investment? Investors invest their money wherever there is profit potential; political systems may have some impact, but investment decisions usually have few loyalties, and certainly not to any one political system, whatever its relative moral virtue.

Democracy is a thought on how people should be governed, and it is a system of government that has gained increasing popularity during the past two hundred years. Whatever the form of government, if that form is the choice of the people, then it is democracy in reality. On the other hand, market economy is an economic reality, developed and evolved according to people's needs. The western market economy may have been impacted by many other factors, but in general, it is an economic reality and the application of the theory of the firm. The two are different, and while sometimes they come together in a marriage of convenience, they are certainly not a match made in heaven.

Sometimes, though not often, it is obvious, that the political system has nothing to do with economic performance. The following statement is a case in point:

> Democratic institutions have often been mere ornaments in the social life of the advanced capitalist nations: proudly displayed to visitors, and admired by all, but used sparingly. The places where things really get done — in such core institutions as families, armies, factories, and offices — have been anything but democratic. Representative government, civil liberties, and due process have, at best curbed the more glaring excesses of these realms of unaccountable power while often obscuring and strengthening underlying forms of privilege and domination (Bowles and Gintis, 1986: 4–5).

Democracy and Entrepreneurship

Democracy has very little to do with the development of entrepreneurship. There is clear evidence that some democratic countries have developed among their people an overly government reliant mentality, in effect, discouraging entrepreneurship. There are countries with good social welfare schemes designed for the common good and to assist less fortunate people through difficult times. These schemes work well for a large number of people, but more frequently, some people developed a government reliant mentality, unwilling to seek new employment nor risk the unknown to start up new ventures. There is also evidence that democratic countries which consider education (all levels of education) to be a citizen's right rather than a privilege, and heavily invest in education, turn out a large number of university graduates with postgraduate degrees who tend to be interested in working for the government or large corporations. The reason is: why should anyone spend twenty years (or more) of time and energy to start up their businesses only to face uncertain returns?

There is other evidence to prove the form of government has at best a secondary effect on economic development in many democratic countries as compared to those less democratic ones. One may be shocked to see that the less democratic countries have high and very high economic growth, whereas the very democratic nations have very low or even negative economic growth. Now the high growth countries are also typically less developed countries with large populations of low wage earning workers but what all this says is that these effects are much more important than the form of government. Many of us may recall not too long ago, how Hong Kong's police force smashed the colony's street vendors' entrepreneurial spirit by kicking and throwing their goods and stands all over the streets over a long period of time. The incident did not kill their entrepreneurial spirit, but it merely reflected a colonial governing reality. Is this the same spirit that has been contributing to Hong Kong's economic success? It is anybody's guess, but it is a case in point that the political system has very little to do with entrepreneurship. Some people have questioned: "Why is UK's economic performance so poor when it can produce Nobel prize winners such as J. R. Hicks and James Meade?" One passerby who heard the query explained: "Simple. UK may have produced many intelligent people but the country has been cheated by its own medicine." Unfortunately, we do not know.

Entrepreneurship is a matter of mindset and it is a natural ability possessed by every individual by virtue of birth. The rest is all environment of which the political system is only one element. Entrepreneurship may flourish under any political system. Even in the former Soviet Union, entrepreneurs existed and created wealth, but the state took the wealth from them. Therefore, the real issue of entrepreneurship is ownership and equity. Equity need not be money, but passion and love as well.

2

Energy, Energy Flow, and the Theory of the Firm with its Impact on Business Management

The origin of everything in the planet earth is no other than the planet itself which is part of solar energy. Therefore, we are energy ourselves. As energy is creative by virtue, obviously, we are creative by birth. Since the essence of entrepreneurship is creativity, everyone of us in this world possesses an entrepreneurial drive within ourselves.

A Branch Grown from the Roots is Stronger than a Branch Grown from Another Branch

It is not the intention of this book to deal with economic theories. Nevertheless, we must look into the theories of economics because if entrepreneurship is to be meaningful to people, it is necessary to inquire into its origin. By tracing back to its roots, we will have a better appreciation why the idea of entrepreneurship has achieved its current status. I have been largely prompted in this endeavour by a wisdom that the late Professor Kierstead of the University of Toronto imparted to me during his last days of teaching.

I recall that I was the only student under him studying the "Theory of Profit". He gave me a reading list some twenty pages long, but to my surprise, the list contained not a single work of his own. Like any other student, naturally, I wanted to know my supervisor's work, benefit from his thoughts, and share his wisdom (of course, I also did not wish to be terribly different from his ideas, as this might affect my performance). I asked him, "Why are none of your works in the list?" He was in his sick bed and said to me: "Raymond, to study the 'Theory of Profit' is a serious attempt. I am afraid if my work is listed on the required readings, you will read only my work, and pay less attention to the works of others. If so, your work will be built on top of my work. Like trees, when a branch grows on top of another branch, it will be a weak branch. On the other hand, if you inquire into the origin of the economics discipline, you will be like a branch growing from the roots, or closer to the roots, which will be a strong work." The lesson I learned from this particular incident has benefited me throughout my life. For this reason, I have decided that my early attempts on developing my thoughts in this book should start from the roots of the tree, the origin of all happenings.

Energy: The Origin of All Origins

Anthropologists and paleontologists can easily verify that life began long before human beings in our present form. Similarly, human history began long before there were any written theories of economics, even though economics is the natural father of organizations, in particular, business and business management.

Following the idea of using energy to understand how economics and entrepreneurship work, it is not difficult to appreciate that every human activity, including thinking, crying, loving, violence and/or engaging in business activities involves the flow of energy.* Energy can be used both to create and destroy. Ordinary people engaging in business activities provide jobs, create wealth for the individual and add value to society. On the other hand, countless energy flows are harmful to humanity, including killing others for personal satisfaction, and doing business with the intention of merely making profit and endangering life support

---

* Based on the idea of "business is energy flow" advanced by Professor Kenneth Kao (the author's son) of Memorial University, St. John's, Newfoundland, during a casual conversation with the author in respect of the "origin" of all human endeavours.

to all living beings. For this reason, energy flow is always being managed: controlled, regulated, channelled or at least, monitored or directed. The real challenge is how to control, regulate, channel and monitor the energy flow in the interest of humanity now and in the future. In terms of entrepreneurship development, it will be a twofold challenge. The challenge to the individual is to self-cultivate, nurture and develop his own entrepreneurial spirit despite unfavourable factors that may affect the entrepreneurial mindset, and to create a favourable environment that induces entrepreneurial spirit through societal and organizational efforts.

Conformity: A Killer to Entrepreneurship

A child plays with garbage, it is in every aspect, an evidence of the flow of energy: the child activates his brain by using his hands, and co-ordinates his brain and hands, wishing to create something that he considers to be of wealth to him and of value to the parents (to show his parents that he is doing something of value). If the parents appreciate the value that the child attempts to create, they should encourage the child to complete his creation, even though what he creates may be objectionable to them. However, most parents prefer their child not to play with garbage. What they are likely to do is to tell the child: "Don't play with garbage; if you want a toy, we will buy you one." This incident is a simple illustration of how energy flow (playing with the garbage) can be interrupted by an external force. Instead of encouraging the child's creative instincts, they have stifled them, perhaps even worse, made the child become more dependent on the parents. On the other hand, a child who does not listen to the parents but continues playing with garbage, will most likely be viewed as a problem child by others.

The following is another striking example that illustrates how conformity is a hindrance to an individual's creativity.

A kindergarten teacher asked pupils in her class to draw a bear and to colour it. All the children did their drawing and coloured it either in brown or white (some with no colour were presumed to be white) except one child who coloured his bear green.

The teacher was surprised, and told the child: "Jeffrey, there are brown bears, white bears but not green bears! Where did you get the idea that the bear's colour is green?" A few other children in the class laughed, and the child, appearing to be a little withdrawn, replied to the teacher: "I like green. Green is beautiful, it's good for us." The teacher then told the child to sit down and re-emphasized to the whole class: "Children, we have brown bears and white bears, but we do not have green bears. Remember, the bear's colour should be brown or white, but not green." All the children in the class responded with a loud: "Yes", except the embarrassed child who coloured the bear green.

The teacher was right. Based on the established standard, the bear's colour should be brown or white. The teacher could not accept that something could be different from the generally accepted practice. A practice is generally accepted because everyone can identify with it. While brown or white are accepted colours for the bear, green is not because people cannot identify themselves with the bear's colour being green. On the other hand, the child, in his response to the teacher, clearly reflected his inherent pleasure for the environment by stating that green is good for us. Why did the teacher not accommodate his initiative and explain to the other children why he perceived the colour of the bear to be green? What is the price of conformity?

The author's brother-in-law, an internationally well-known painter, paints fish climbing up trees and people ask him: "How can the fish climb trees?" He replies: "People can invade the water, why can't the fish climb trees?" After all, humans and fish share the same earth. If humans contaminate the water and kill all life support, why is it so wrong for the fish to climb trees? Incidentally, we have never troubled ourselves to ask the fish how they feel about the way we invade and contaminate the water and kill all their life support.

The three illustrations are not in themselves unique, but the message is clear: though men are creative creatures by virtue of birth, the entrepreneurial spirit (creativity and innovation) can be lost through learned behaviour in the home environment, through the educational system, or due to social context. Obviously, homes, schools, and society are establishments. The priority of any establishment is the orderly conduct of the individual; that is, conformity. The sad thing is that conformity is not the best atmosphere for the encouragement of creativity as it is spurred by the need for change. When the last Chinese dynasty was overturned, the numerous revolutions that followed denounced Confucianism because it represented the establishment and conformity in many aspects of the Chinese culture. It would not have made any sense for these revolutionary movements to permit the people to follow the teachings of Confucius, who was viewed as the defender of the old establishment. In the revolutionary view, new approaches to social order were essential. Similarly, teachers of today who preach to would-be entrepreneurs about the need for eliminating risks may also kill initiative in the process.

The Mystery of Equilibrium

The world never stands still; the universe is dynamic. The same applies to humans, human activities and the environment. Yet economists claim there is such a thing as equilibrium. What is an equilibrium? In the simplest possible terms, it is a state of constancy. Economists also admit that given a long enough time, everything is variable. Therefore, there is no real equilibrium. Nevertheless, the concept is useful because it allows us to define how we are now, and thus how we want to be. In other words, the concept of equilibrium is a device which allows us to examine our current state, so we can make changes (disequilibrium). We must realize that in our attempt to acquire a desirable state of equilibrium, we must initiate a disequilibrium. This process reflects nature as a state of constant flux. We must appreciate that nothing stands still; we either live and progress, or allow ourselves to deteriorate, decay and die. A more oriental viewpoint embraces the concept of harmony rather than equilibrium, and of the cyclical nature of the universe. In this viewpoint, our spirits will be reintegrated with the universe (or pure energy) and flow again as part of pure energy. Unfortunately, this is an area which we know little of.

Inasmuch as the concept of equilibrium is contrary to nature, economists nevertheless make it work for economic analysis. On the basis of the results generated from this analysis, procedures are constructed: this has led to the establishment of standardization and creation of professionals, and professional organizations. Human activities are then controlled through the standards of professionals, and standardization and professionalism, the champion of the status quo, are enemies of entrepreneurship.

Standardization and Professionalism

Standardization and professionalism are mechanisms created by people who made themselves the Establishment of society. They do so collectively, through organizations such as law societies, the college of surgeons and physicians, the institute of chartered or public accountants, or the institute of chartered financial analysts. In fact, in virtually every human activity, so long as it may affect another human being, there is a governing body created to enforce conformity of professional practices. Educational institutions are no exception. What is ironic is that our educational institutions are created supposedly to develop individuals to make changes, so we can all live long and prosper.

In my recollection, when our elder son was five years old attending kindergarten in a local primary school, he never really was happy to go to school, and we did not know the reason why. One day, we received a call from the school's vice-principal who said: "Please come to the school, your son's teacher wants to speak with you." I went to the school, rushed to the kindergarten class and noted my son was placed in a corner of the gym (it was used for class when activities such as dancing, and singing are involved), lying down flat on his back with his two arms stretched on both sides as if he were dead. I asked the teacher why was he lying down and not playing with the other children. She said to me: "Your son is restless; he is different from the other children. He is a troublemaker in class. I suggest you send him to a special school." As a teacher in a post-secondary institution, I knew more or less how special schools operate: a child sent to a special school must have some problem, that is, he does not conform to certain standards. I did not think I could achieve much with the teacher so I went to see the principal. The first thing the principal said to me was: "What is the problem?" I stated the fact that my son was being treated differently and asked him to look into the matter because the teacher described him as a troublemaker. I asked him what my son had done. He said to me, "A troublemaker is a troublemaker. We are the professionals; we know what we are doing." I really did not wish to argue with the professionals, but I was also in the teaching profession, so I said to the principal: "Would it be possible for you to assign my son to another class, and see if he is the same?" The principal was good enough to accommodate my request. I took my son home and kept him at home for a few days just to lessen the shock of changing classes and teacher. A week later, my wife took him back to school, but to another class. After two weeks, I visited his new teacher who told me, "We have no problem with your son." Our son went through the school system with virtually no difficulty or problem of any kind to our knowledge. His interest is in science; he has obtained his PhD from a world class university and published more papers than I. As a researcher, he has developed himself in a number of world renowned institutions, including the University of Cambridge, and he is now holding a tenure track appointment with a professorial rank at a well-known university in Canada. While this was merely a personal experience, nevertheless, it strikes me in this way: This particular "professional" incident could have damaged an individual's potential. If I had gone along with the professional advice to send my son to a special school to correct his non-conforming behaviour, what would have happened is really beyond my perception.

Although there are exceptions, hardly any surgeon in the world would use an innovative approach that deviates from the established procedures to operate on a patient. There is also hardly any accountant who will prepare a financial statement that does not conform with the generally accepted accounting principles. Nevertheless, it is a known fact that to act contrary to the established professional standards can result in a penalty that is truly fearful: from a minimum of submitting to a disciplinary inquiry, to the suspension and termination of one's professional practice.

Unfortunately, to ask a true professional person and a professional body to be innovative and to initiate changes would almost be like putting a camel through the eye of a needle. It is possible, but the camel must be killed first, decomposed into a liquid form and pulled through the hole.

Very much like the legal profession where laws only recognize change and, if not never, seldom initiate it, it is possible to make changes within a given profession, but it will only happen after a lengthy process. In the first place, the initiative must come from an individual through research and publication, and brought about through lengthy discussion and exposure in committee after committee. The end result is more often than not unpredictable. For example, although there have been countless individuals, including professional accountants themselves attempting to recognize opportunity cost (foregone revenue, such as, a person leaves a highly paid employment to create a new venture and receives no adequate compensation similar to the remuneration received from the previous employment), in accounting practice opportunity cost as a part of operational cost is still in limbo. However, it would be unfair if the difficulties confronted by professionals who practise their professions outside of prescribed procedures or guidelines are not stressed. For a surgeon performing surgery outside of prescribed proven operational procedures, the consequence can be unthinkable. The damage could be from law suits against both the surgeon and the association (licensing body), to a criminal charge of manslaughter if the patient died after the surgery, even though the death had nothing to do with the surgery. Similarly, if an accountant prepares financial statements deviating from the generally accepted accounting principles, it would make the information difficult to communicate with other users who are familiar with the professionally (meeting the professional standards) prepared financial information. On the other hand, there are also people who are totally disenchanted with the level of control exercised by the professional organization over others in the same profession but not members of the organization. For example, one frustrated individual at an open forum of an international conference made some comments about professionalism, and referred to professional organizations as establishments created to protect self-interest. This remark was immediately responded to by an elderly European professor who said: "Sir, don't you forget, it is the Establishment that provided you with the good living you are having today."

Just as the European professor said, the Establishment provided us with the good living which we never had before, and conformity will make you successful forever. If you do not believe it, just listen to what some people say about Japan. In Japan, if you are a graduate from Todai, this in itself is instant success. Todai is the university which produces political leaders like a wholesale market. The corporate executives of

Sony and Honda have come from the Todai ranks as well. But do you wish to find out what Todai graduates' recipe for success is? You may be surprised to know it is not academic excellence. "The Todai formula for success is one part examination brilliance, one part old boy's network, and one part conformity to a dead end orthodoxy" (Gray, 1993: 52). This will probably help you to solve this mystery: why there has been no one from Todai who won the Nobel prize on account of his success. Obviously, examination brilliance, conformity and the old boys' network would not help you to win a Nobel prize, but it has certainly helped Japan make a lot of money, both for the country and the individuals. Of course, the success of Japan the nation as a whole is not quite as simple as that. The motivational factor for Japan's success will be further examined later.

Professionalism and standardization have, for better or for worse, filtered into almost every inch of our lives, and over into the educational institutions which are supposedly places to explore the unknown. They use standard texts (such as my own), standard teaching modes, standardized tests and examinations, and of course, standard answers (scored by the computer). A paper which does not cite others' works less than sixty times (a number used to prove a point) may not be considered as scholarly work, even though two well-written paragraphs may serve the same purpose. The whole world (or at least the well-to-do countries) seems to believe that individuals ought to be trained, told and sometimes forced to conform to standards made by others. All these may be for the good of better living, but there is one question that needs to be raised: if everything is to be standardized, what will happen to the individual and individual initiative? How will change take place? Will the future world be entrepreneurless, or will entrepreneurship be just for the birds?

If everything is to be standardized, we would need no one to run the world. All we need to do is build a dream computer and write the software to run it. Computers are better than humans at everything but adopting and creating. In a fully standardized world this will be unnecessary. Our quality of life will be totally determined by the standards we have programmed into the computer. Is this the world we want? By the way, should it be the case, I would assume that only those who created this world could possibly be Nobel prize winners, and the last winners at that, but the trouble is who would be left who could make that decision?

Although standardization and professionalism have taken a stranglehold on all human endeavours, they cannot yet standardize the individual's thoughts and mindset, even though they do limit them. Perhaps then, there will only be so much that professionalism and standardization can do to stifle energy flow, as long as we hold the individual's thoughts to be sacrosanct and the efforts that science and research take to understand them are usually off limits to professional organizations. Unfortunately, the same is not applicable to disciplines in the humanities and social sciences, including those disciplines that serve the business world.

Technological Evolution Versus Making Changes in the Humanity-related Disciplines

Change in the disciplines of technology and science, and change in the humanities are quite different, particularly in the business and business management-related fields. This is largely because of the degree of control or regulatory measures levied in the respective disciplines. Whereas the acceptance of scientific findings is largely based on quantifiable measures, in the case of business-related disciplines, professional organization approval is usually required (see Table 2.1). For example, a new power source that replaces the combustion engine in power automobiles is by all means a technology breakthrough, but to ask accountants to ignore stock exchange commission requirements for preparing financial information would be next to impossible, because of the need for standardized financial reporting. Perhaps this is the reason why we have advanced so much in technology, but less so in the field of management. It may come as a surprise that little has changed in the field of organizational and business management for the past fifty years. The post-World War II period (in the early 1950s) saw the development of the ideas of management by objectives, and a few years later, through the management control system, came goal congruence (congruence

Table 2.1

Comparing the process of making changes between the field of science and technology, and humanity-related disciplines

Individuals initiate the change	Idea formulated on the basis of individual's perception for changes	
	Science and technology	Business-related discipline
Idea testing	Laboratory: sample testing (controlled by the researcher)	Solicit opinions: from people (influence by others)
Expose tested results	Feedback from peers for further improvement and/or modification	Feedback from peers through publications and individuals
Decision for commercialization or implementation	Based on the merit of the product	Based on the acceptance of the professionals

with the goal of the firm, not the goal of the firm in congruence with the individuals in the firm). Then through management accounting the profit centre concept came along, and then team work, and now, some forty or fifty years later, these old soldiers have not died, they have not even faded away.

The best idea of the past two decades has been "intrepreneurship", a half-brother of entrepreneurship which failed the blood test of acceptability because the whole excitement of being an entrepreneur is ownership, and without ownership, intrepreneurship is no more than giving the concept of profit centres a new coat of paint. Looking at technology, can anyone dispute its advancement? The changes are taking place not only from decade to decade, but from year to year or sooner. In the business-related management discipline, *In Search of Excellence* (Peters and Waterman, Jr, 1982) came to the market in the early 1980s, creating a lot of excitement, with its action and people approach, and ideas such as: "management by walking around" and "fire, aim" style of business management. After a few years of honeymoon, however, there has been nothing new or different. If we compare this to the changes in computer technology, it is not surprising to realize how much standardization and professionalism have hindered the progress of humanity science, particularly business, and the business management disciplines. We stress the importance of professional managers and professional management associations, when the truth is that the most professional management is management by computers. If this is so, why do we need managers at all? We may go so far as to accept professionalism in management, but we should never accept professional managers, because the true professional managers have to be computers.

Theories of Economics as Related to Entrepreneurship

The creative process originates with an individual. The individual may abstract from massive information available to him, then sort, organize and make the information meaningful and develop it into a theory or idea (see Table 2.2). Theories are not developed by groups, mass majorities or organizations. They have been and always will be the brainchild of the individual. Today, ideologies in economics may have flown in all directions, but their origin, to a large extent, is based on a single publication: the *Wealth of Nations* by Adam Smith, the founding father of classical economics.

Those of us who have had the opportunity to explore the *Wealth of Nations* would easily appreciate Adam Smith's principle: the factors of production are land, labour and capital. If this were indeed the case, and

Table 2.2
The theories of economics at work

Theories were developed by the individual through the following process:	
Activate energy	Abstract thinking: to bring the universe into the area of the human body so the brain can operate
Monitor energy flow	Abstract information gathered from abstract thinking, sorted, analyzed and organized in a logical fashion
Channel energy flow	Use deductive reasoning to see how to organize information, store in the individual's brain and apply it to reality
Determine energy flow pattern, and establish a theorem	Apply the theorem to human activities

if he were living today, he would have a hard time placing Singapore in his theory since with virtually no land or natural resources, without even adequate fresh water, the people of Singapore have created a thriving nation mainly through their entrepreneurial efforts.

The old master did a great deal to shape our economic behaviour, through his emphasis on the labour theory of value. It came with two extreme offspring, capitalism and socialism (with communism, the extreme of extremes) (see Table 2.3). Karl Marx's capital theory stole the limelight for at least three-quarters of a century (since 1917) and caused the loss of millions of human lives, made life miserable for hundreds of millions more, and caused the misallocation of trillions of US dollars of natural resources (wasted on war and other misallocations). It ended with the downfall of the Soviet Union, and the rest of the world watched as the members of what was then the Soviet bloc joined the capitalistic ranks. Unfortunately, those countries operating under the capitalism banner are not really doing that well either. Both ideologies nevertheless come from the same root, the economic theory that has dominated us during the past and the present and will, more than likely, dominate the future.

Today, socialism still exists, but it is in many ways a walking corpse which does not know enough to lie down. Capitalism has shown its cracks reflected in the deep recession faced by countries like the US, the UK, Canada and Australia. In fact, other than in a few countries in the Pacific, the recession virus is being spread across the rest of the world. Therefore, if socialism is now a walking corpse, it would not be too far-fetched to consider capitalism as the "walking wounded".

Classical economists may not have done much to cultivate or nurture entrepreneurship in the interests of humanity. It was an economist who

Table 2.3
Economic theories, empirically tested if possible

Macro		Micro	
General population as organized groups Economic policies		Individual as an agent for wealth creation	Firm as profit-making unit
Socialism	Capitalism	Profits belong to the entrepreneur, a reward for hard work, risk-taking and managerial competence	Profits belong to the firm, a reward for capital investment
Economic activities determined by the group in a position to make decisions for the general population	Market economy: Economic activities are tested in the market through (1) the acceptance of a firm's product or service at a preferred exchange value; (2) Capital supply to support the firm's need for growth	Supported by accounting practice via ROI	

christened the entrepreneur as the organizer for the factors of production; a second-class citizen in the economic doctrine, after land, capital and labour and it sometimes seems that this attitude has not changed in 250 years. It is not the intention of this book to dig up graves to beat up the dead, recognizing that the dead cannot defend themselves. But the fact is that classical economists have never appreciated that it is the process of entrepreneurship that creates wealth, not labour. On the other hand, why should a 250-year-old ghost be blamed, while even at the tail end of the twentieth century, people are still puzzled as to what entrepreneurship is and who an entrepreneur is.

The neo-classical economists had done even worse than their forefathers in ignoring the importance of entrepreneurship. Through their brainchild, the theory of the firm, and the building of the mathematical model for economic analysis, they drove entrepreneurship out of circulation in the economic doctrine for nearly a century. Even though Joseph Schumpeter made a great attempt to rescue it from the dungeon, the professional accountants had already made their claim to quantify the conceptual word "profit" into dollars and cents, thus making the theory of the firm a living giant in business through the use of the magic words: rate of return on shareholders' investment. However, it would be unfair to ignore Jean-Baptiste Say (a French industrialist who ran a spinning factory) who caught the spirit of entrepreneurship and gave it a home. The entrepreneur, as he perceived in his doctrine (1803), is a coordinator, and supervisor of production (functioning in the factory). It was this Frenchman who distinctly made the entrepreneur the fourth agent in the production process equal in importance to land, capital and labour. In his idea of human industry, labour's operative role was clearly separated from the role of the organizer. It was also the first time in economic literature that the risk-bearing nature incorporated in the entrepreneur's role played a part in the production process of economic doctrine.

The Theory of the Firm and Entrepreneurship

For our economists, it is like hitting a home run if the theory of the firm is mentioned. The theory of the firm tells us why firms exist, and led the way for the recent development of management science, and accounting practices that stimulated capital accumulation. The bottom line approach to business management, and the theory of the firm has to be credited for its contribution to industrial growth and the expansion of firms. It is the godfather of economics if not forever, at least for now and possibly well into the twenty-first century.

What is the magic of the theory of the firm? The magic word is "profit", although few people can really appreciate the meaning of profit. As someone once said: Economists can tell us a lot about profit, but they can never show us what profit is. On the other hand, accountants can show us all kinds of profit but we view them with suspicion.

In the theory of the firm, a firm is considered to consist of a group of homogeneous individuals, and it is entrepreneurless. As Baumol (1968) put it, the Prince of Denmark has been expunged from the discussion of Hamlet. As homogeneous individuals, the firm is assumed to be an entity that behaves rationally in the interest of the firm, and the interest of the firm is no other than satisfying the goal of the firm: profit, and maximization of profit. Conceptually, since the firm consists of homogeneous individuals, then every individual in the firm should have the same goal of the firm, that is, the maximization of profit for the firm.

On the basis of this theory, discussions among a large number of writers seem to concentrate on the various expressions of what profit is. Profit can initially be defined as revenue minus cost. If profit is to be maximized, it is logical to assume that the firm must do what it can to maximize revenue on one hand, and minimize cost on the other. Hence model builders started to build models to satisfy this assumption, despite one missing ingredient: people, the entrepreneur in the first place, and in addition to the entrepreneur, the host of others who might be working in the firm. Under the assumption that everyone in the firm has the same goal as the firm, therefore, the goal of the entrepreneur is also profit and profit maximization. It is a convenient assumption that makes any other consideration disappear like a magician from in front of a large audience. However, it must be recognized that inasmuch as the disappearing act is only an illusion, on the other hand, the magician may say: "Who cares? As long as the idea of profit maximization for the firm works well in the market system, I am happy with it."

With the firm rolling in profits on top of profit, and accelerated capital accumulation that makes the market economy the saviour of the human race, the whole world seems crazy about the idea of market economy, even though some of them have no idea just what a market economy is. Under the circumstances, it would be right to say that the real saviour is not the market economy, but the thoughts behind the market economy which originated from the thoughts of economists and the theory of the firm, and have been transformed into operational apparatus which has made the world that we live in today. From the point of view of economists, what joy and what satisfaction! The interesting thing is, if the market economy is good for humanity, the true heroes are the entrepreneurs. However, they are not the winners of the Nobel prize — the economists are. We should not be surprised since under the theory of the firm, a firm is entrepreneurless. The market behaviour of "entrepreneurs" are not human enough. No wonder at least one Hong Kong newspaper was creative enough to give a title to some "human profit takers" as "criminal entrepreneurs".

The Theory of the Firm and its Impact on Business Management

In terms of relativity, there is no perfection in this world. The theory of the firm may be hailed as the hero of the market economy, nevertheless, it is far from perfect. There is another side of the theory yet to be explored.

As the theory of the firm acts like a godfather to guide economic endeavours, the single most important element of the theory is not in matters of production, or treatment of cost, but the distributive element of the theory. In short, how do you determine profit and to whom does the profit belong?

Long before the theory of the firm established its territory, Jean-Baptiste Say considered the entrepreneur to be the coordinator and supervisor of production, and his share of rewards is the share allocated to the use of "human industry". In the established distributive practice, interest is to be paid for the use of capital, rent goes to the landlord (or the cost of the use of facilities, equipment, machinery, etc.), and wages are to be divided to pay those performing operative tasks, labour and entrepreneur's rewards.

Say also stressed that factors limiting the supply of entrepreneurship (high entry cost, requisite qualities, and random events), accounted for the entrepreneur's usually high returns. Thus, in the entrepreneur's rewards, in addition to considering service as a coordinator and supervisor in the production process, a return on personal investment is also included. However, Say also made it clear that the return on capital investment should not be part of the entrepreneur's remuneration; rather, it is a return to the capitalist for investment. It is clear in his distributive theory that the reward to the entrepreneur for entrepreneurship is quite different from the reward for personal capital investment. In Say's distributive theory, it is clear what the sources of profit generation are, and the entitlement of profit among those involved in the productive and distributive process.

Israel Kirzner (1979; 1986) developed the theory that an entrepreneur is an arbitrageur and an equilibrating agent, functioning in the marketplace. He considered that the entrepreneur's remuneration is a return for arbitrage. The entrepreneur "proceeds by his alertness to discover and exploit situations in which he is able to sell for high prices what he can buy for low prices". Profit, as he perceived, is "something obtainable for nothing at all" (Kirzner, 1973: 48). However, he considered an entrepreneurial decision to take advantage of a perceived opportunity, since such a result may be the continuing cumulative long term strategic decision. In this respect, the gains out of the ordinary productive and selling process are monopoly gains obtained by the entrepreneur from the initial capturing of the monopoly position. For whatever it is worth, Kirzner paved the way for a conceptual argument: Entrepreneurs are motivated by financial gains and, "stimulated by the lure of profits; alertness to an opportunity and on its ability to be grasped once it has been perceived". (Kirzner, 1979: 11).

Throughout the twentieth century, there have been numerous contributions from individuals such as Schumpeter (1934), Cantillon (1931), Knight (1921) and Marshall (1961). According to Schumpeter, profit is a net gain: "it is not absorbed by the value of any cost factor through a process of imputation" (1939: 105). Profit is a residual, an excess over the sum of the factor payments. The profit goes to those who introduced the new combination.

Knight's entrepreneur is an agent who is willing to be responsible for discretionary decisions, a managerial risk-taker in short. Profit is then the reward for exercising the entrepreneurial function.

Marshall's view on the entrepreneur is a combination of various ideas on entrepreneurship. He is a business leader and head of the firm, innovating, coordinating, responding to profit-generating potentials, and bearing risk. He pays the factors according to their respective marginal productivity, and keeps the residual for himself.

Throughout the literature of this period (the late nineteenth century and early twentieth century), the entrepreneur has been viewed as the person who is entitled to the operational residual. Under the theory of the firm, since the firm is entrepreneurless, who will be entitled to the profit? The logical solution would be: if the firm is not to return the profit to government through taxation, or redistribute it to the individuals in the firm, it would be retained in the firm, in a sense, increasing the equity value of the firm. Profit, therefore, will simply melt into the big pot of equity. Equity holders (stockholders) decide what to do with the profit, and in rare cases, may decide to impart some to those working in the firm, but more often than not, the profit goes to the shareholders. The profit might be used for the firm to expand and develop its growth potential. To satisfy the investors' desire for profit, the goal of the firm would be profit, which would satisfy shareholders. This is how the brilliant idea of rate of return on investment became a yardstick to measure business performance.

It is obvious that all inputs contribute to profit, and there will be no profit if every factor receives its full compensation, or its contribution is less than the compensation it receives (see Figure 2.1).

The theory of the firm has done a great deal of good to guide the development of contemporary economic literature. It made it possible to apply theory to business applications, and policy makers use it to form their nation's economic policy. On the down side, it is totally ignorant of the importance of people as individuals); indeed the theory itself makes the entrepreneur, the creator of the firm, disappear from economic analysis. In fact, it made the firm, created by the entrepreneur, entrepreneurless (while the whole idea of democracy is to recognize the individual as "individual", the economists on the other hand, with so little effort through their entrepreneurless firm theory and mathematical manipulations make individuals disappear like the strong wind blowing the dust [individual human beings] into the air).

It is a tragedy for a discipline in the humanities to lose its humanity; that is, for economics to assume that a firm is entrepreneurless. The individual is the principal of all human endeavours, the meaning behind the motherhood words, democracy and market economy, and every-thing that everyone believes in in the western civilization emphasizes the individual. In a socialist state, an individual is not important, but considered only part of the state, and every individual within the state working for the state earns his wages by performing the required task whilst profit goes to the state. Under the theory of the firm, everyone working for the firm earns his wages for his work and profit goes to the

Figure 2.1
A distributive pie under the theory of the firm

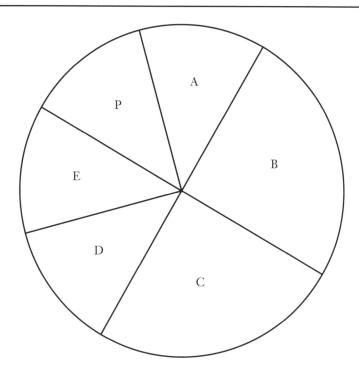

A = Payments to suppliers for goods and services
B = Payments to workers
C = Payments to managers, including entrepreneur's remuneration
D = Payments to the use of deferred assets
E = Payments to taxes levied by the government
P = Profit to shareholders

firm, thereby to the shareholders. The only difference between the socialist state and the market system under the theory of the firm is that under the socialist system, people are working for the state. Under the theory of the firm, employees work for the firm, which represents its shareholders, and therefore, every individual in the firm is working for the shareholders (see Table 2.4).

The greatest contribution of the theory of the firm is that it gives capitalism the conceptual base it needs. This has seldom been noted. A renowned US economist said: "A definition is only as good as its application." The theory of the firm is the conceptual base for capitalism, because under the theory, it is the capital that sustains the firm's

Table 2.4
A firm in a socialist state and under the theory of the firm

	Socialist state	Under the theory of the firm
Ownership	State	Shareholders
Individuals in the firm	Employees of the state	Employees of the firm
Management	Representing the state	Representing the shareholders
Source of capital	Supplied by the state	Invested by investors
Competition for funds	Allocated by people who have the position of power based on the perceived state priorities	Decision is made by investors on the basis of profitability
Employees' remuneration	Determined by the state	Based on a contractual agreement made between the firm (represented by the management) and the employee (individually or collectively)
Profit	Belongs to the state	Goes to the shareholders
Profit computation	Revenue after all costs deducted	Revenue after all costs deducted
Union's position	Cooperate with the state	Representing employees, bargaining with management

development and growth, therefore, the business success exhibited today is the result of financial investment at work. Investors are lured to invest their money into business because of profit. Entrepreneurs are supposedly the creators of the firm, but are nevertheless non-existent. The idea of entrepreneurless entrepreneurs in the firm comes about not because their performance is part of the human industry, but because their skills involve the use of other people's money to make money. No wonder some of our academics claim that entrepreneurship is the pursuit of opportunity beyond the resources under entrepreneurs' control. It is also perhaps for this reason that some individuals also claim that entrepreneurs do not risk anything, but investors do. All of these make a convenient argument that profit belongs to the investors (shareholders), because they are the true risk-takers.

Guided by the glorious triumvirate of the market system, capitalism at work, and the rate of return on investors' investment, managers (including CEOs) of firms are able to benefit from employing the cheapest possible input, from the cheapest of the cheapest, the environment, air, water, land, then oil, and other fuels and labour. With these cheap inputs, they provide a lot of people with a high standard of living, and make a lot of profit for the firms and their investors. In the name of profit, an entity can justify itself by razing the Brazilian rain forest. They chop down the trees, drive away the natural inhabitants to provide pasture to raise their cattle for slaughter, and proudly announce to the world: "Last year, we served the world over one billion hamburgers."

As profit maximization becomes the goal of the firm, every individual in the firm is supposed to have the same goal as the firm, hence every individual is expected to contribute to the firm's profit which dictates the entire management strategy. A simple justification in the marketplace is that all firms compete for the same funds and unless investors are satisfied with their investment return, they will either cease to invest in a particular firm, or as an extreme measure, pull out their investment (by selling their holdings cheap) altogether.

Through fear of losing the investor's (or shareholder's) trust, the management of the firm would do what it can to drive the operation toward achieving profit. It is no surprise at all then, that managers of the firm are constantly watching the firm's stock price in the stock market. Whilst the stock prices are monitored, so are all the employees' performances. If the employees' reason for working is to earn a living, what they must do is to work hard to make money for those investing in the firm.

As the goal of the firm is to make profit, accountants have transformed the abstract term "profit" into a measurable quantity: the rate of return on the investors' investment. This is a magic term which dominates most business management practices. It is the philosophical basis of corporate strategy.

As an added credit to the theory of the firm, by making a firm entrepreneurless, it has made another landmark achievement which is seldom noted: the separation between people and the firm. In a later stage of development, we will witness another piece of magic: the creation of the management profession by separating business management from the firm's ownership, which is the conceptual base that made the general management model, the dragon-like workhorse for business in the twentieth century and possibly beyond.

3

Profit, the Motherhood in Business: Can It be the Messiah for Humanity?

When a fisherman catches a fish, he is as well off at the end as he was at the beginning. The fisherman makes a profit, so who makes a loss?

Capital: The Most Pampered Fat Cat in the Market Economy

Before inquiring into profit, it might be just as well to start with a brief exploration of the word "capital". Why not? Karl Marx made his mark this way and even after his death half of the world remember him as a devil, while the other half still think of him as a saviour of the working population.

Capital, as I see it, is the most pampered fat cat in the market economy. Russia, a country under Marxism for close to a century, once

34

it turned its back on Communism, received aid to the amount of US$3 billion given by the G7. It was not as an investment with the expectation of returns, but an investment to reward those turning their back on Communism (call it "decommunizing") and joining the capitalist rank (*Time*, 19 July 1993, 12). Even after the "white house" incident where people were killed and protesters were arrested, for fear of Russians favouring Communism again, the G7 pumped in more support (not only moral support but also material support), so Russia could fulfil its capitalist dream. Maybe one day, as claimed by Russia's leader Boris Yeltsin, Russia will join the elite, and the G7 will become the "G8". China, on the other hand, is still a Communist country but has developed a new ideology to practise market economy within the socialist system: opening its doors and inviting private investors from all over the world to invest in China. Now, regardless of how others feel about China's way of practising market economy, so much capital has flowed in that it looks as if the Yellow River has broken its floodgates. It is not the author's intention to make a political comment, but the puzzle is that whilst China remains a Communist state practising a market economy, and attracting significant private sector investment from all over the world, Russia, on the other hand, is practising market economy under the democracy banner, and requires substantial financial support from the western governments (more specifically, the G7). I suppose it is all capital at work, but it clearly means different things to different people.

Although capital is generally perceived as money, capital is not money itself, but the resources we use money to acquire. Resources are needed for life support and for producing goods and services.

Resources include everything from land and anything buried underneath it, air, water, plants, and everything that we make or move, including the total environment which we employ to produce goods and services for sale, or facilitate other forms of business transactions. All resources are limited in supply. Economists throughout the centuries have said much about the scarcity of resources, yet to this day, there has been nothing to account for the real cost (to build into the cost structure for generating sales, thereby, profit) for the use, waste, abuse and killing of these resources at our disposal. How much is the real cost for air, water, industry waste, or endangered species? Is there any accounting system for the dumping of waste that makes the environment in some places uninhabitable? Is it true that economists and accountants care only for accountable dollars and cents? What is the cost of depleted mines? What is the cost of contaminated lakes? China, a country with four thousand years of human history, has plenty of fish in the waters and lakes anywhere you go. On the other hand, in the much younger countries such as North America, there are fish unfit to eat, water unfit to drink and air unfit to breathe. Much of this damage has occurred in the past five decades. However, with China's desire to undergo rapid industrialization, what will happen to its environment is anybody's guess. The question is that if we use up most of our capital the way we are doing now to our environment, will there be any profit for humanity? Capital is like a workhorse; if we kill or injure the horse, where then is our profit? A fisherman catches a fish, he is not as well off at the end as he was at the beginning, unless the fish he caught spawned its eggs, and there is a continuation of the fish population.

Profit: The Motherhood of Business

A group of young people were disenchanted with the modern society: They scorned profit, they despised businesses, they preferred not to get jobs because they deplored the nine-to-five routine. In fact, they hated the whole monetary system. They gathered in Vancouver and then journeyed to South America where they found an island that appeared to be unpopulated. They started their new life, independent of the rat race, in as primitive a way as if they were back in the Stone Age. At first they were quite self-sufficient. Eventually, however, they felt the need for various things and subsequently employed some simple technologies, including the building of a dam for irrigation and the making of a few new tools. An exchange system followed and bargaining began. Bargaining is a price system. And the price system brought about profit and loss. So once again, profit appeared among the disenchanted (Kao, 1984: 65).

While the whole world is crazy about the market economy and capitalism, it would be foolhardy to attempt to impose a universal definition of profit. The truth of the matter is that profit, used so frequently by us, is perceived differently by different people. In fact, profit is a conceptual word. Economists have tried all they can, but to this day, no one has successfully been able to tell the world: "Here is what we mean by profit." J. R. Hicks, a Nobel prize winner in Economic Science made his name by defining profit as when an individual is as well off in the end as he was at the beginning (Hicks, 1950: 172). His definition has been simplified by the author for illustration. While economists play with words, accountants on the other hand, play with figures. First, there was profit; then, financial income. This was not quite right. So, next came rate of return on investors' investment, then, rate of return on assets, and finally, residual income. Once a frustrated man who could not quite grasp what economists wanted to say, nor appreciate what accountants wanted to do, said to his business colleagues: "I'll tell you how I feel about profit. Economists' profit is playing with words, and accountants' profit is playing with figures. To me, profit is playing with money: the more money I can make, the more money I can have, the more profit there is."

When the question of profit is addressed to the environmentalists, they will tell you: "There is no profit." Where is the profit? In the name of profit, we are razing our forests, ruthlessly killing harmless animals for their body parts and in the name of sport, depleting everything that can be extracted from underground, catching fish before they can spawn, and dumping chemical wastes into the water which is necessary for life support. Under these circumstances, ultimately no one makes a profit, even if one person or firm appears as well off in the end as at the beginning. On the other hand, it really does not matter how economists play with words, accountants play with figures, business persons play with money, or how environmentalists scream out loud wanting profiteers to have a heart for the environment. Profit will always be the centre of attention, but profit cannot be derived unless capital remains intact. Therefore, the challenge, at least for us in the jungle of profit, is to honestly face reality and measure capital accurately. It is also perhaps the reason why many firms making a sizeable profit as reported through their financial statements, are unable to distribute any cash profit, for fear the dividend paid out will not be part of the profit, but part of the capital. So the question is not the issue of determining the meaning of profit, but rather how capital can be accurately measured and maintained.

To measure the capital change between two defined times called a beginning and an end (as required by Hicks' definition) is, to the economists, next to impossible. In the first place, capital represents all forms of input (including natural inputs such as air, water, and environment, utility performed by equipment and other forms of capital assets), therefore, it is illogical to aggregate every capital element into a single input. Capital is used for the purpose of production, and production is a circular process; once it begins, it will go round and round without an end. Similarly, in business, while capital is always needed, without knowing the production period, it would not be possible to determine the exact amount of capital used, and without knowing the exact amount of capital invested in the production, there is no way that profit can be precisely determined. Perhaps, conceptually, it could be possible; if a firm terminates its operation, then there will be an end and profit can be determined. On the other hand, in today's business world, is there anybody crazy enough to shut the door of the business, count the profit, then start all over again? Although the idea of a complete shutdown of the business to determine a production period serves Hicks' definition well, transforming this into operational terms still involves measurement problems. Therefore, even though the idea of "being as well off in the beginning as at the end" makes sense, for the economists, this is still a very nebulous concept. It is no wonder that some people say economists can tell us all about profit, but they cannot show us profit. Incidentally, although this is a matter of great concern, at least one very practical concept arises from Hicks' remarks about profit that an individual must observe: he said that it cannot be profitable (in his sense) to make machines unless the use of the machines is also profitable. Therefore, in order to assess the profitability of an investment, we should look at the production of the final product (Lindbeck, 1973). This fundamental truth can be extended to include a concern for our environment: No undertaking can be profitable for any business, unless the undertaking is profitable to our environment, or at the minimum, harmless to our environment.

Different Profits from Different Activities

There are other economists, such as the late Professor Kierstead, who believed profit had no singular form (1959: 1–3, 12, 22, 25). To borrow his version of profit, the author took the liberty to expand profit into the categories in Table 3.1.

There is no need to elaborate on the first five categories in Table 3.1, but what are "gains from heaven"? They could be anything from money or goods found (as long as no one makes a claim) in the street or fallen from the sky. Nevertheless, for those of us wanting life to be simple without complications, it might be easier to throw out all these analyses;

Table 3.1
Categories of profit

1. Operating profit	Residuals generated from business activities in the normal cause of operations
2. Visional profit	Gains from working on the entrepreneurial vision, a visional reward through the pursuit of opportunities beyond the normal business conduct.
3. Windfall gains	Gains from changes of nature, not controlled by human beings
4. Speculation gains	Gains from speculated future event but with no visional base
5. Contributory gains from societal advancement	Gains from societal advancement, the firm had no measurable or visible contribution
6. Gains from "heaven"	(See main text)

who cares what profit is, as long as there is money that lawfully belongs to us? Alternatively, you may be satisfied with the following story:

> Once upon a time, there was a well-dressed man preaching to a mass gathering. Everyone was impressed and moved by his sermon, and all of them were willing to make a sizeable contribution to heaven through him. In those people's minds, they were making an offer to heaven. But one bystander asked him: "How are you going to offer this money to heaven?" He replied: "I shall offer this money to heaven by throwing it above; heaven can take what it wants, and what falls on the ground are gains for me from heaven."

Profit Means Different Things to Different People

Entrepreneur's Profit

While presiding over the first Canadian National Conference on Education held in Toronto in 1990, I noted a distinct dissatisfaction among some of the participants over educational institutions. There was at least one person at Workshop No. 6 (The Environment for Effective Learning) bitterly attacking teachers for not understanding what the free enterprise system was, and for teaching students nothing about making money. Obviously, the mood at the workshop tended to assume that entrepreneurs are people in business for the purpose of making profit, and profit is money. As a teacher myself, I of course had much to say about this, but I did not interfere with the discussion, since as the president of the conference, my role was not to get into an argument with the participants. But I was puzzled and to be honest, I was disturbed.

One year later, I was invited as a speaker at the First Chinese Entrepreneurs World Conference held in Singapore. When it was just about time for my presentation, one participant from South Africa was very aggressively advancing his disenchantment to a number of academics discussing entrepreneurship. He protested: "I have spent a lot of money to come here to be treated as a schoolchild and have academics tell me about what entrepreneurship is. I came here because I want to know how to make more money. I want to make more money and I want my children to learn how to make money, so I send them to a country where people can teach them how to make money. I want my fellow countrymen here to tell me how you have made your millions and billions of dollars, so I can learn from you. I am not interested in listening to professors talk." (This is not a direct quote, but taken from my own notebook.) The audience (approximately 800 to 900 participants) burst into laughter.

I suppose being a professor myself, I could not help but feel insulted. So, when my turn came to give my talk, I asked the chairlady to give me the privilege to respond to his remark. I said to the audience: "Yes, I know you want to make money and have more money; so do I. You may use money to do a lot of things you want, including using money to buy your freedom, but I am sure, you will not sell your freedom for money."

These two incidents made me feel very uncomfortable about how much, through education and interaction with one another, the meaning of entrepreneurship has been distorted (the topic will be dealt with in a later chapter), and the entrepreneurs' perception of money, profit and the purpose of the pursuit of entrepreneurial endeavours has changed.

Profit is not only about dollars and cents to entrepreneurs. The objective of going into business means different things to different entrepreneurs. For some people it may even be a passion for a product or service they have successfully developed, and for others it may be because they wish to do something for their country. Although profit has been used as a measuring tool, profit to an entrepreneur is an achievement, the achievement of desired visional outcomes. In a sense, this is real profit. The real profit is represented, for example, by an increase in physical assets, the residual from employees' contribution, the ability to compete and pursue growth opportunities, goodwill, good working relationships among individuals in the firm, availability of disposable resources, an increase in communication skills, networking, and among other things the achievement of personal goals such as providing employment for the entrepreneur's children, or a comfortable living for the family, and/or social status. Of course, some people might argue that all of these can be measured by money. Then, do we measure interpersonal skills, good human relations and goodwill created by the entrepreneur engaged in business undertakings in dollars and cents? It should be noted that inasmuch as an entrepreneur may use money to buy all inputs (other than his own personal sacrifice), create the business, engage in business operations, and determine revenue generated from business activities, he can never measure profit accurately, because profit cannot be aggregated.

It should be noted that in Figure 3.1, a part of profit (A), that is, dollar profit, can be negative or a loss. However, if (B) is greater than (A), the entrepreneur's firm is still making a profit. This may be true even in the event that the loss in (A) is so great that the firm is in financial difficulty, and subsequently fails. If (B) is sufficiently great, the entrepreneur can still use the residual to start up another business. This is the reason why some entrepreneurs are able to start up a business again even though they suffered from their earlier attempts.

Figure 3.1
An entrepreneur's profit

Revenue (assume it has been correctly measured through accounting process) represented by dollars and cents

−

  Input expensed to generate the above revenue

Input can be purchased   +   Entrepreneurs' personal contribution
by dollars and cents   including reasonable living allowance, and
                                          other personal sacrifices which cannot be
                                          measured accurately by dollars and cents

=

  Profit

(A) Represented by   +   (B) Residuals of: goodwill; networking;
    dollars and cents   human relations in the firm; developed
                                            skills in communication, etc.; surplus of
                                            employees' contributions; and others

---

Investor's Profit

Contrary to an entrepreneur's profit, an investor's profit can be determined in dollars and cents. It is therefore a realizable financial profit determinable by accountants. Table 3.2 shows the simplest way to illustrate this point.

Table 3.2
An investor's profit

Sold investment holdings, net realized cash	$100,000	
Minus: Cash investment	60,000	
Book gain		$ 40,000
Less (add): Market price fluctuation		
at the time of disposal	(500)	
Commission	400	
Opportunity cost @ 5%	600	500
Profit (measured by dollars and cents)		$ 39,500

Alternatively, profit can also be determined by a stock analyst to relate price with earnings (see Table 3.3).

Table 3.3
Investor's profit determined by price-earnings ratios

ABC Inc. earnings per share as per analysis		$ 6.00
Price = approximately 5 times its earnings according to analysis = $6 x 5 = price per share according to stock analyst		30.00
Purchase price at the time of purchase		20.00
Book profit per share		$10.00
Less (add): Price fluctuation at the time of disposal	(1.00)	
Commission	0.05	
Opportunity cost	0.20	(0.75)
Investor's profit		$10.75

Accounting Profit: Let the Figures Do the Talking

While economists are troubled with having no way to show what profit is, accountants are much more realistic about the challenge. Since life must go on and no one can wait forever, therefore, whether there is a good definition to be applied for a practical situation, or a proper treatment for different profit, as practical minded professionals, accountants work their way around by dividing the profit according to an accounting postulate (the period convention). So long as the board of directors of the firm agrees with the operational period and it is acceptable to the inland revenue authority for taxation purposes, an operating period can have its beginning on the first day of any month, and end at the end of another month covering a period of 365 days. So long as everyone follows the practice, no one cares whether or not it is possible to determine the production period.

On the basis of accounting postulates, two examples are used to illustrate how accounting profit (or net income) is derived.

Illustration 1: The Invisibles

Assume that an entrepreneur (who fits the wealth creation and value adding definition) developed an automotive computer, to record and evaluate all aspects of a car's performance, which could be attached to any printer with a specially designed interface also designed by the entrepreneur.

With some personal savings and "love money" (from parents and in-laws), he started his own business and employed family members plus a few required outsiders. In view of the company's restricted cash position, the owner had done extensive "scrounging" to provide the needed equipment, simple machinery, tools, and vehicles for the business. Assume that the following values (verified by competent professionals) were assigned to each of the assets. These include a five-year-old van (with 20,000 km on the odometer) valued at $10,000 (the value of a new van would be about $40,000), various tools, machines and electrical appliances, purchased either from scrap or second-hand dealers at a cost of $10,000 (total value if new, $50,000), and some other equipment taken from his workshop at home valued at $5,000 (total value if new, $50,000). In view of the cash position, the entrepreneur and his family agreed not to receive remuneration for at least three years. Family living expenses were to be paid from the entrepreneur's wife's salary, received from a college where she was a teaching master. If all family members were to be paid for their work at the business, the total payroll would be as shown in Table 3.4 (based on salaries and wages for similar jobs at fair market value).

Table 3.4

The entrepreneur (chief executive officer)	$ 80,000
His wife (helping on week-ends)	20,000
The entrepreneur's son	30,000
The entrepreneur's daughter	30,000
The entrepreneur's mother-in-law	40,000
Total human resources at market value	$200,000

To start the business, the entrepreneur invested his lifetime savings of $50,000 and a cash gift from his parents of $50,000. The opening balance sheet of the company and its operations after one year (1991) are shown in Tables 3.5 and 3.6.

Table 3.5

Assets		Liabilities and equities	
Cash	$100,000	Common shares	
Van	10,000	(at no par value paid for	
Tools and electrical appliances	10,000	100,000 shares)	$125,000
Equipment	5,000	Total liabilities	0
Total assets	$125,000	Total liabilities and equity	$125,000

Table 3.6

Sales		$600,000
Cost of goods manufactured:		
Material	$100,000	
Direct labour*	150,000	
Overhead**	150,000	
Total	400,000	
Less: Ending inventory	42,000	358,000
Gross margin		242,000
Less: Commercial and administration expenses***		125,000
Operating profit		$117,000

*   Wages and salaries were paid to non-family employees. All members of the family, although they worked as direct labour, received no remuneration for their contribution.

**   Including depreciation expense for the following:

Van $10,000 @ 30%	$3,000
Tools and electrical appliances @ 20%	2,000
All others @ 10%	500
Total	$5,500

***   No remuneration was paid to the entrepreneur himself, or his wife who assisted him in managing administrative details (including handling the company's bookkeeping and other office functions). This does include a general manager's salary of $50,000 and an accountant's fee of $5,000.

The company's financial statements, although not officially audited, were prepared by an outside accountant and were considered as properly reflecting the company's operating result, and in accordance with general accepted accounting principles. There were no other notations or explanations beyond the required data. The situation was similar the next year. The company's financial performance (before income taxes) for the two-year period was as follows:

1991	$117,000
1992	$133,000

On the basis of the company's financial performance and the amount of equity commitment provided by the owner/manager, the bank manager granted the company a line of credit for an amount sufficient to meet the firm's cash flow requirement. The line of credit included an initial loan of $25,000 at the end of its first year of operation. However, during the third year of operation, a number of things happened:

○ The owner/manager's wife left him. Hence, he could no longer rely on her income to support the family and had to hire an outsider to assist him in administrative duties, at a salary of $50,000.

○ The owner/manager exhausted his savings. Even though he realized that the company faced a cash flow problem, it was necessary for the company to compensate his administrative efforts, so he started to pay himself an annual salary of $70,000.

○ His mother died on New Year's Eve.

○ His mother-in-law was no longer interested in working in the factory. In fact, he and she were no longer on speaking terms.

○ The elder child left home to live in a university residence about 400 kilometres from home, and the other child (who normally helped in the factory) left home on a Pacific tour with a few of his friends.

○ The old van broke down and the owner/manager had it removed from the premises. The cost of towing was greater than the scrap value, but the garage man decided to call it even.

○ The bank manager extended the firm's borrowing to a ceiling of $80,000, mainly because the company had to purchase two new machines, some tools and electronic equipment, and a computer for the factory.

○ The city fire inspector visited the company and ordered the owner/manager to move the plant elsewhere within six months for fire safety reasons.

As the result, the company incurred the following costs in its third year of operation (see Table 3.7).

Table 3.7

Owner/manager's remuneration	$ 70,000
Additional labour @ $25,000 x 4	100,000
Salary for the administrative assistant	50,000
Additional payroll tax and other variable overhead associated with additional payroll requirement	70,000
Total	$290,000

In addition, the company was faced with other cash pressures, including bills accrued from the purchase of the assets in Table 3.8.

Total additional operating costs for the third year were $330,000. There would be additional costs (not yet incurred) for moving to another location within the period allowed by the fire inspector.

Table 3.8

A new van	$40,000
Two new machines @ $36,000	72,000
New tools	20,000
Computer, including software	15,000
Total additional cash outflow	$ 147,000

   To furnish the needed cash, the owner/manager mortgaged his house for $150,000, but this was not sufficient to meet all cash obligations. In view of his honesty, additional investment in the company and good relations with the bank, his bank manager extended his borrowing limit to $120,000 in January 1993. In March 1994, the company was unable to meet interest payments to the bank and payables due several months before. The third year's operating result was obviously going to be a loss. If the owner/manager required additional financial help to move the plant, he would have to supply the bank manager with audited financial statements, which would show a loss of approximately $250,000, with a moderate increase in sales over the last year of about 10 per cent. Of course, the bank manager could refuse further financing and decide to recall the outstanding loans to the company. In that case the situation of this company would indeed be grim.

   After observing the above, one cannot help but question the accounting concept of profit (accountants prefer to use the term income rather than profit): Why did the firm have annual sales of $600,000 to $700,000 for the first three years but experience no change in the actual cost structure, and employ almost the same input? Why had it made a profit of $117,000 and $133,000 in the first two years, and yet expected to incur a loss of $250,000 for its third year's operation? Of course, there are answers to these questions. There were substantial invisible contributions toward the production and operation of the business, not accounted for in dollars and cents. Under these circumstances, can the figures really do the talking?

Illustration 2: Profit, No Profit or the Same Profit?

In late 1988–89, Toronto (Canada), Atlanta (USA) and a few other cities entered into bidding for the 1996 Olympic Games. Most Canadians' assessment was that Canada's bid should be favoured by the voting members of the Olympic Committee. Not only is Toronto renowned for its cleanliness, it has shown its support of sporting activities through the success of its club franchises, including the Toronto Blue Jays, currently the most successful team in major league baseball both on and off the field. Every facility reflected the spirit that would make the 1996 Games a real success. However one NDP (New Democratic Party) city councillor opposed the idea of hosting the Games, because in his opinion, Toronto could better spend its money on social welfare rather than by putting it in sports competitions. Nevertheless the Canadian Olympic Committee submitted its bid for the honour.

Toronto, like any other North American city in the late 1980s, was on the edge of a deep recession, but the city fathers (people who make decisions for the citizens of Toronto) and other Canadians all had high hopes for Toronto to host the Games. The high expectation generated a surge in opportunity-driven entrepreneurs and would-be entrepreneurs. George Simmon and Susan Wu, two young university graduates, were among those opportunity-driven individuals. Both George and Susan were working for multinational corporations. They were, however, always interested in the pursuit of market opportunities and dreamed of having a business of their own.

In discussing the matter with Patrick, George's brother, the three felt strongly about the idea of starting a business then with the expectation of Toronto hosting the Olympics, as a stepping stone to bigger ventures. Patrick said the undertaking could give them the experience they needed, so the three formed a partnership incubating a business essentially producing and selling Games' souvenirs. As the host city had yet to be determined, they thought of using a suggestive approach to design the merchandise, rather than waiting until the Committee came out with the decision. Patrick had already designed a series of products, including a T-shirt, sweat shirt and mugs. Patrick's designs focused on the Olympic colour, but not the symbol, and he combined it with images of the multicultural environment featured in Toronto. As a test of his work, he submitted his design to a design award competition, and to his surprise, he won the top prize.

Motivated by this initial success, the three proceeded with the undertaking. As an initial attempt, they purchased a batch of white cotton T-shirts from Pakistan which looked simply brilliant with Patrick's design.

They produced and launched their first batch of "look alike and feel alike" Olympic T-shirts in the market. The undertaking was funded by $60,000 "love money" from their parents, their savings of another $60,000 and a bank loan of $80,000.

The initial response from the market was very favourable. Through Patrick's networking, they were able to push the product into most of the gift shops in Ontario and Quebec. It was simply good. Table 3.9 shows the first month's operating result, prepared under a standard costing system suggested by an accountant.

Table 3.9

Brilliant Enterprise		
Revenue 50,000 T-shirts @ $5.00		$250,000
Manufacturing cost* $3.00 x 100,000	$300,000	
Less: Ending inventory	150,000	
Cost of goods sold		150,000
Gross margin		$100,000
Less: Commercial and financial expenses		40,000
Net income		$ 60,000

* Including salaries of partners working in the factory and other production-related fixed
  costs of $60,000 based on a standard capacity of 100,000 units.

In July, the partners decided not to produce any T-shirts pending
the outcome of the Olympic Committee's decision. There was no change
in sales.

The partners were very uncomfortable about the operating results for
July (see Table 3.10). Patrick, in particular, was concerned. He said to
his partners: "Since the sales were the same, we all worked in July and
costs were all the same, why is it then, in June, there were sales of
$60,000, but nothing for July?" Susan was more sensible about this. She
explained to Patrick: "Patrick, if we take two months together it would
be the same. The trouble is in the inventory."

Although Patrick was not fully convinced, he asked whether there
was any other way of calculating the operating result. He was told by
Susan that if the contribution approach was used, the results would be
better presented. She proceeded to write her calculations as shown in
Table 3.11.

Table 3.10

Brilliant Enterprise Operating Statement for July 1988		
Sales		$250,000
Cost of sales (standard)	$150,000	
Underapplied fixed cost	60,000	210,000
Gross margin		40,000
Less: Commercial and financial expenses		40,000
Net income		$ 0

Table 3.11

	June	July
Sales	$250,000	$250,000
Variable cost		
50,000 x $2.40	120,000	120,000
	130,000	130,000
Less: fixed cost	60,000	60,000
Manufacturing margin	70,000	70,000
Less: Commercial expenses	40,000	40,000
Net income	$ 30,000	$ 30,000

George was impressed but puzzled, and asked: "We need $3.00 to produce one T-shirt, why do we only count it as $2.40?"

Either of the preceding methods is acceptable, but why is it then that there were different net incomes if the methods used were different? Which one should be the profit?

The Residual Income

According to accounting practice, a residual income can be derived by deducting a capital charge from an accounting income calculated under any method. Using Brilliant Enterprise as an example:

Month of June — accounting income	$60,000
Capital charge based on $120,000 @ 1%	1,200
Residual income	$58,800

The idea of using residual income to determine profit is an attempt by accountants to bring accounting income closer to economic profit. But it is still far from real profit.

It would not be a surprise if some people were to remark: "Yes, accountants can show us all kinds of profit, but we don't believe them." Then, whose profit should we believe? Accountants or non-accountants? Economists or non-economists? The frustrated business person may say once more: "Who cares, a profit is a profit."

4

The Rate of Return on Investment: Is It the Guardian Angel for Capitalism, or Demon to Humanity?

If a lily pond contains a single leaf on the first day and every day the number of leaves doubles, when is the pond half full if it is completely full in thirty days? The answer is the twenty-ninth day. There is increasing concern among many thoughtful people that humanity is in the twenty-ninth day of its stay on Earth (quoted by Fredric P. Sutherland in the Foreword of Clifton and Turner, 1990).

The Rate of Return on Investment (ROI)

There are many wonders in this world, but none of these wonders is as powerful or influential as the concept and practical use of the rate of return on investment (ROI). This simple arithmetical manipulation has been on the centre stage of our business world for a long time. With the socialist world shifting its paradigm in favour of capitalism, the rate of return on investment will most likely stay with us as long as there is such a thing as business, and business is done through business entities.

The rate of return on investment is a fairly straightforward concept. In a broad sense, it is a measuring tool of the financial performance of a firm which encompasses both optimal financing and the effective and efficient use of investment to achieve the goals or objectives of a firm as assumed by economists under the theory of the firm, although not everyone clearly appreciates the difference between effectiveness and efficiency. Charles T. Horngreen (1965) illustrated the point by saying "the killing of a housefly with a sledge-hammer may be effective, but it is not efficient." Accountants are able to illustrate the difference using the expressions:

Profit/Sales = Profit in sales (efficiency)   (A)
Sales/Investment = Turnover (effectiveness)   (B)
(A)/(B) = Rate of return on investment   (C)

The rate of return on investment embraces both the need for achievement of a desired objective and the drive for optimization between input and output. It is therefore used widely as the financial goal of a firm and the focal point of the corporate financial executive in developing financial management strategies to maximize the equity holders' rate of return on investment (Kao, 1986: 1).

ROI, Capital Market and Business Management

As a profit concept, ROI is being widely used not only as a measurement for a firm's financial performance, but also to induce investment. It is the latter concept that made ROI the single most important ingredient for the development of capitalist society as we know it today.

The ROI concept induces investment, and investment supports business growth and expansion, therefore, ROI is in effect the engine behind economic growth, and the guardian angel for capitalism. Without it, there is no adequate measurement of the firm's performance, and investors have no means to know what to invest. From the point of view of a firm, ROI is used to ensure that resources under the managers' disposal are effectively and efficiently used. To public investors, ROI is the bottom line blessed by the stock exchange (capital market), as through listing requirements and disclosure practices it allows investment analysts to make their living by advising their clients how to invest and get their desirable return on investment (see Figure 4.1).

Figure 4.1
ROI, capital market and business management

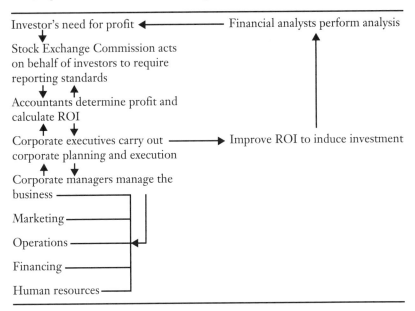

The determination of the rate of return on investment is based on profit and investment, and the determination of profit and investment are the responsibility of accountants. To a lesser extent, it is the Stock Exchange Commission that monitors how accountants calculate the profit and investment (unless the Stock Exchange Commission and accountants as a whole do not do their job well). In other words, if the Stock Exchange Commission is disenchanted with the accountants' concept and/or method used to derive profit or investment, it is the stock exchange's responsibility to intervene. Alternatively, it may decide to act independently of the accounting system (to avoid this unfortunate possibility, the professional accounting organizations involve representatives from the stock exchange in the accounting standards setting process), or invite government intervention. The following two statements reflect this point.

Statement 1   The following is how Professor Edward Stamp perceives the goal of the US Stock Exchange Commission:

> ... to have the American equivalent to the French commercial code. They will admit that they do not trust management and they do not trust accountants. The more details that can be written, the less these people can play around (Seidler, 1986: 7).

Statement 2

> In my judgement, as long as business corporations and other institutions in
> our society have external accountabilities, reporting standardization is here to
> stay. The extent of standard setting depends on the economic environment
> — turbulent times will demand more standards than stable times. Without
> economic stability, GOVERNMENT intervention is likely to increase.
> Instability encourages regulation of economic behaviour. Instability multiplies
> financial reporting problems. A stable economy is the best way to prevent
> standards overload (D. Kirk, President, AICPA, quoted in Hepp and McRae,
> 1982: 62).

While Professor Stamp's remark reflects how accountants feel about
the Stock Exchange Commission and its power to influence accounting
practices, Mr Kirk's statement signifies the possibilities of government
intervention.

If, therefore, it is the ROI that drives the business managers in the
firms, it is the Stock Exchange Commission's power of intervention that
sets the rules of the game. Hence, inasmuch as people tend to think that
under the market economy, a firm's operation is driven by the market
(market driven), at the operational level of the firm, it is the decision
makers, CEOs and managers of the firm who are constantly seeking
ways and means to acquire needed capital to support the firm's growth
and expansion or pursue market opportunities. Therefore, the economy
is really capital driven, be it in the marketplace, boardroom, or educational
institutions. Why educational institutions? Because these are the places
where a large number of potential CEOs and general managers of
business entities come from.

The theory of the firm, the theories of management, and the framework
of general management are bridged by the rate of return on investment.
In this way, they form a triumvirate which, in the eyes of the business
world, is virtually untouchable (see Figure 4.2).

Management Theories, ROI and the Theory of the Firm

Management Theories

In business, action is everything because of necessity, but in the academic
environment, everything begins from theory. Management theory is
considered by some to be a science, by others an art, and by still others
to be both. The practical necessity is that management is a way of life,
and as long as there is humanity, there is a need for management.

Figure 4.2
The rate of return on investment and its relationship to the theory of the firm,
the theories of management and the framework of general management
(a general management model)

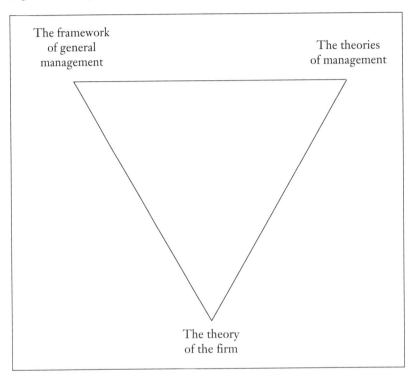

Management theory provides us with a framework to judge our actions and a basis from which to implement change.

Understanding resources is popularly viewed as the key to successful management, but people with real management experience recognize that the key is really understanding people. The founder and then CEO of Consumer Distributing Ltd, once told the author, "Raymond, when you are in my position, you will know all the time spent on the job is to find ways to motivate people, people, people; that is what management really is." Despite the fact that under the theory of the firm, people are separated from the firm, people should always be the "star" of business. But this was not in the mind of these management experts who developed those glorious theories that have influenced both practical business management and the educational process.

There are four major groups of management theories (see Table 4.1). Classical management theory embraces scientific management and bureaucratic management. As advocated by Frederick Taylor (1856–1915), scientific management aims to standardize work methods and use rational selection of employees coupled with training and job development to achieve efficiency. Bureaucratic management was praised by Max Weber (1864–1926) as being the way to deal with management challenges for large corporations such as General Foods, IBM and Standard Oil. The model organizes massive numbers of people in complex situations. The bureaucratic model relies on multiple levels of reporting to divide responsibilities and control resources. The unfortunate result is often a pyramid of committees and subcommittees, endless paper work and meetings, meetings and more meetings.

The more sensible group of management theories stresses the importance of human relations. It is a good thing somebody thought about the people working in business. This movement has been the result of the efforts of a large number of individuals and has made a remarkable impact on management theory and practice. The bottom line is still super performance in the attainment of the goal of the firm, but human beings now receive a significant share of management's attention.

Systems theory came along with the advancement of technology. Theorists in this stream advocated that a system is a collective association of interrelated and interdependent parts. Machines and technology are part of our systems, but systems are defined by relationships among people. The systems approach provides a frame of reference for managers who must make decisions in a constantly changing environment.

Contingency management suggests that managers should prepare to adapt their leadership role to accommodate different situations. On the other hand, it is also part of the theory that managers should be assigned to situations that best fit their leadership style.

There are also other management theories, including the recently developed quantitative management theory which is represented by management science, operations management and management information systems. There is also the Type Z theory group, an American adaptation of Japanese management practice, which focuses on the improvement of management toward employees' interests with measures such as long term employment, improved benefits, and most important of all, concern for employees and their families. The idea of concern for employees and their families is a good one, except there is still a fundamental difference between Japan and the United States. In Japan, management efforts are devoted to developing individuals as members of the family, but in the US (and possibly other countries), management efforts tend to develop individuals as employees.

Table 4.1
Summary of management theories

Name of theory	The theory	Who's who
CLASSICAL	Scientific management	Frederick Taylor Lillian and Frank Gilbreths
	Bureaucratic management	Max Weber
	Administrative management	Henri Fayol

BEHAVIOURAL
GROUP
	Human relations: better
	  relations, better
	  performance
		Chester I. Barnard
		Kurt Lewin
		Mary Parker Follett
		Elton Mayo

	Theories X and Y	Douglas McGregor
	Motivation theories	Abraham Maslow
	Integration theories	Victor Vroom Lyman Porter

	Theory Z
	  American adaptation of
	  Japanese organizational
	  behaviour
		William Ouchi

SYSTEMS	Contingency theories	Frederick Luthans
QUANTITATIVE	Operations management Management science Management information systems	The use of computer technology, model building, and mathematical manipulation

The Theory of the Firm and the Theories of Management

The theory of the firm was adopted by people who needed a conceptual base to challenge Karl Marx's *Das Kapital*. Capitalism is labelled by communists as a vampire which sucks the blood out of the working population. Now the Berlin Wall has been torn down and Communist and Socialist regimes have fallen all around the globe, capitalism has experienced a worldwide resurgence. All of a sudden it has become a universal panacea which will bring wealth to all. In this capitalist Utopia, people will enjoy the same standard of living everywhere, and the price and availability of goods and services will be the same in France, Thailand,

China, Costa Rica, Reunion Island, or the Ivory Coast. The puzzle is, will the practice of capitalism really do all this for us? This is the trillion dollar (here again, money and capitalism) question. Unfortunately, the dream of equality is never part of capitalism, therefore, it is pure speculation. Nevertheless, no matter how we state it, equality or no equality, capitalism or no capitalism, the name of the capitalist's game is still a matter of management.

We have a lineup of management theories used to build models and to guide actions which have to be applied and implemented by people. All theories and models are developed on assumptions, and the management model and theories of management assume that the firm is an independent entity. It is an assumption derived from the theory of the firm, and if the origin is to be traced, the credit should be given to Adam Smith. To appreciate the development sequence, we begin with Adam Smith's open market concept, through the theory of the firm, then the general management model and the accountants' efforts to turn theories into the goal of the firm measured in terms of ROI designed to satisfy capital holders' (shareholders') expectations (see Table 4.2).

Table 4.2
Sequential development of theories in economics, management, the general management model and ROI

Development sequences	Theories and practices	Utility
1	Adam Smith's open market economy: The market is governed by supply and demand	The founding of classical economics
2	The theory of the firm: The firm is an entity, the firm's goal is profit maximization, individuals in the firm have the same goal as the firm. The theory separates people from the firm making the firm entrepreneurless	Made it possible for the development of business management into a profession. It induces the development of management theories
3	Theories of management: The goal of the firm is profit maximization. Management is a function in the market economy, and management resources need people to achieve the goal of the firm.	As the basis to build models; guide for actions

Table 4.2 (cont'd)

Development sequences	Theories and practices	Utility
4	The general management model: Advocates the notion that a firm is an entity, management to be separated from ownership, a profession specializing in managing other people's business. The model amplifies the need for the awareness of management theories, skills and techniques required to manage a business. These include the core of business management, the tools required to manage, knowledge about business functions, skills and techniques needed to manage resources and deal with people, to plan and control. General management encompasses planning, organizing, staffing, leading and control for the attainment of the firm's goal	As the basis of curriculum development for business management education and guide for action
5	Strategic management: Management in action, mapping out goal attainment strategies within available resources and the existing environment	To activate theories and models through action and managing
6	Rate of return on investment: An arithmetical calculation that bridges profit, the theory of the firm, theories of management, general management model and strategic management. Its universality stands worldwide	A simple tool to measure a firm's performance which made capitalism a living giant that dominates the capitalistic economy

The Scope of General Management and the "B" School

The general management model is built on the basis of the need to guide management practice, or perhaps more appropriately, to guide business management education. There is no precise general model that will satisfy all, but there is a general direction which varies in accordance with the model builder's perception of what is needed to turn an individual into the general manager of a firm whose function is to manage according to the goal of the firm. Business schools ("B" schools), within the university environment, are institutions designed to develop individuals to fill the managerial posts in businesses and/or various organizations including government (see Figure 4.3).

Figure 4.3
Scope of general management

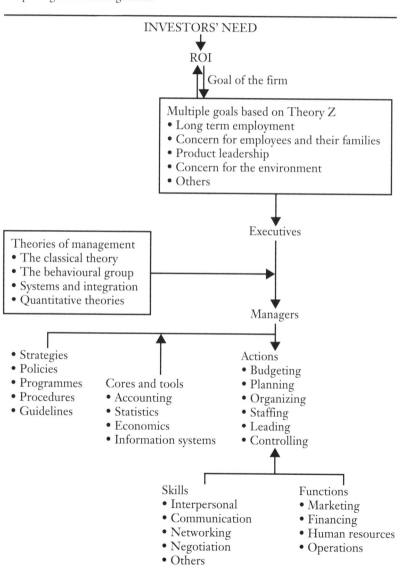

Historically, in the early part of this century, perhaps it was at the Pennysylvania University that the first "B" school, the Wharton Business School, was created, thus paving the way for further development of "B" schools in universities today. It should be noted that the objective of the Wharton School at that time was to train the younger generations of the rich for the purpose of taking care of their family businesses. "B" schools today have been developed into higher learning institutions designed primarily for individuals to manage other people's businesses (see Table 4.3). Therefore, the influence of ROI displayed in business management is similarly found in business schools in the university environment.

Table 4.3
A general management model as seen in "B" schools' curriculum leading to the degree of MBA (applied generalist) or in an area of specialization*

	Subjects	Objectives
Core**	Management principles	General awareness
	Marketing	Knowledge
	Organizational Behaviour	Knowledge
	Economics	Knowledge
	Operations	Knowledge
	Financing	Knowledge
	Accounting	Tool
	Systems analysis	Tool
	Computerized information	Tool
	Skills: Communication	Basic skills
	Interpersonal	
Functional	Marketing management	Managing
	Human resources management	Managing
	Financial management	Managing
	Information management	Managing
	Technology/innovation management	Managing
	Small business management	Managing
	Entrepreneurship	Managing
	Strategic management	
Specialization	Auditing	Specialization
	Taxation	Specialization
	International business	Specialization
	Capital market and investment	Specialization

* Only some subjects are listed. There is a great deal of variation from university to university, but they all begin with core subjects, then functional subjects and subsequently enter into an area of specialization.
** Some core subjects can be electives based on the student's interest in an area of specialization.

The assumptions of the general management model are:

1. Business management is separated from business ownership. The business managers work through the firm but for its owners, the shareholders.
2. Profit belongs to the firm, and the firm is held by its owners, the shareholders. Therefore, profit goes to the shareholders of the firm.

Rate of Return on Investment: Is It the Guardian Angel of Capitalism, or the Killer of Humanity?

There is no question about what ROI has done for capitalism. The issue is whether the continuing push for a more prosperous society and materialistic gains will eventually drive people further apart, leading us to ruin and ultimately kill humanity.

The Power of ROI: Can You Squeeze Blood out of a Stone?

ROI works both for potential investors and for internal performance measurement. Let us illustrate how internal performance measurement works. Assuming it is used to evaluate performance within a division in a large firm where the manager's responsibilities include division profit.

Firm DP has ten product divisions, and a division is organized on the basis of the profit centre concept which has the following characteristics:

- Operational independence
- Has a separate account for cost and revenue
- Managers can act independently in the marketplace
- Inter-company or inter-division transfer with transfer pricing system
- Managers of the division have division profit responsibility

The company's controller's office, authorized by the CEO, establishes the rate of return on corporate investment to the division at 20 per cent, and the capital charge (comparable to an opportunity cost of funds invested in the most secure investment project) at 10 per cent. Divisions are from a to j. Based on the above, the controller's office has a performance chart plotted, as shown in Figure 4.4.

Figure 4.4
The performances of DP Corporation's various divisions

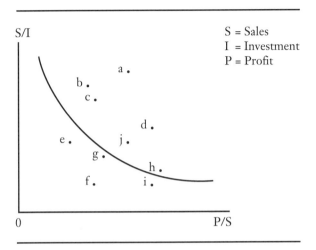

It is obvious that the company expects all divisions to perform along the ROI curve. Those divisions whose performance is below the ROI curve are identified and those above or on the curve are set up as models. As all divisions' performances reach the ROI, the controller then proposes to push the curve upwards (see Figure 4.5). The incentive is to please the investors so they will not pull their money out to invest somewhere else.

Figure 4.5
DP Corporation's expected division performance

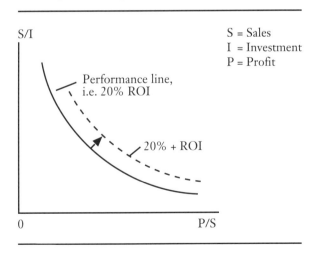

The method is commonly used in large corporations. The theory behind the practice is that if a firm is to effectively and efficiently use its resources, all investments must yield the same return. If not, the investment must be moved elsewhere to give the desired rate of return (the application of equal-marginal theory advocated by managerial economists).

There is another situation that the author himself experienced when working for a large multinational corporation. At a budget meeting, the GM (General Manager) gathered all division/plant managers into his office to assess all units' past performances. One unit manager reported a very favourable performance and indicated that the labour performance had actually achieved standard requirement. Here was what he reported at the meeting: "Our cost analyst and engineers established our theoretical labour cost to be $10.00 per unit, with 10 per cent standard allowance; our standard cost per unit is $11.00. In the past, our performance was always in the range of actual cost being 9 per cent higher than standard, about $12.00 per unit. During the past two months, we managed to reduce our actual labour cost to about $11.20 to $11.40 per unit."

After he submitted his report and explained what happened, the efficiency expert immediately reacted by saying: "Well, why is our standard cost so high? I am going to revise our standard allowance to 7 per cent above the theoretical cost." The manager of the unit was terribly upset and reacted: "Look, we really worked as hard as we could to achieve this performance; people in the plant are expecting some bonus for their performance, but now you want to reduce standard allowance. What are you trying to do? To squeeze blood out of a stone?" The efficiency expert replied without hesitation: "Under the competitive pressures we have to. If there is blood in the stone, then we will just have to squeeze it."

Another incident occurred while the author was working in a steel company as a production planner. It was during a management–union negotiation that the frustrated management outlined the company's financial condition and emphasized the need for a better understanding of what the company was offering. He said to a union representative: "Please be reasonable, we have given everything we could including our hearts, what else do you want?" The union representative said to him: "Keep your hearts, they stink!"

The rate of return on investment is used by virtually every manager. The performance of every manager is not evaluated yearly, but monthly or even weekly. One large department store in North America uses a gross profit test related to each department's investment. The departmental managers are in effect measured on a daily basis, because gross profit testing occurs daily. Similarly, managers of large firms whose stocks are actively traded in the stock market have their performance measured with changes of the stock price of the company, again, on a daily basis.

Everywhere you go, there is this common expression: "Under global competition, we will just have to do everything we can to ensure our shareholders are happy about our performance. Otherwise, we will be squeezed out of the financial market, and we might as well be dead." It is the managers' responsibility to do whatever they can to ensure the shareholders are happy with the firm's performance, and to provide their expected return on investment. Under the pressure for better financial performance, even though their conscience is to do the common good, their priority will most likely be redirected to the shareholders' satisfaction both on bad days and good days. On bad days, this may involve, for example, laying off people as is happening now even among the more properous countries like Japan. On good days, there is the continuous pursuit of opportunity to tax, exploit and damage the environment in the interest of satisfying the shareholders' desire for better return on their investment.

ROI: Is It a "Demon" to Humanity?

As the environment is the silent partner of business, in the name of meeting consumers' needs and wants, capitalism, profit and the rate of return on investment, some ruthless business people are in fact repeatedly raping the environment (for example, through excessive fishing, depletion of non-renewable resources, razing of rain forests) and stealing from the future for the present. If we continue to do so without concern for humanity, it is frightening to imagine the consequences.

There is a well-known riddle posing the following problem:

> If a lily pond contains a single leaf on the first day and every day the number of leaves doubles, when is the pond half full if it is completely full in thirty days? The answer is the twenty-ninth day. There is increasing concern among many thoughtful people that humanity is in the twenty-ninth day of its stay on Earth and that we have little, if any time left to set things right (quoted by Fredric P. Sutherland in the Foreword of Clifton and Turner, 1990).

Even more frightening,

> Pollution and depletion of natural resources are occurring on a vast and historically unprecedented scale. The worldwide use of fossil fuels has increased ten times in the twentieth century, and the atmosphere now contains

25 percent more carbon dioxide than it did in 1900. Each year 200 million tons of sulphur dioxide and oxides of nitrogen are added to the atmosphere (Fredric P. Sutherland, in Clifton and Turner, 1990: xv).

What will happen to our world if the trend continues?

And the future doesn't look promising. By the middle of the next (21st) century, the world's population is expected to increase from the current (1990s) five billion to ten billion. By that time, the world economy is projected to be five to ten times as large as today's $3 trillion. It is going to be difficult in the extreme to achieve a cleaner, or healthier environment in the face of the threats to our natural resources implicit in these projected population increases and vast economic expansion (Fredric P. Sutherland, in Clifton and Turner, 1990: xvii).

Politicians and the media advocate the pursuit of economic growth for all countries and applaud when it is achieved, but honestly, what is the social cost and cost to the environment of this remarkable economic growth?

The rate of return on investment is the guardian angel of capitalism; but it is also the number one killer of humanity if it continues to push for growth and expansion at the cost of the environment.

Accountants are the originators and chief advocates of the use of the rate of return on investment. Now, when the whole world is so concerned about the future of our environment and humanity, it would be fitting for accountants to spearhead an entrepreneurial initiative and contribute to the future of humanity by including the cost of the environment in the cost of doing business before deriving the firm's profit and the rate of return on investment.

5

Entrepreneur, Entrepreneurship and Why Intrepreneurship Failed its Blood Test

Entrepreneurship is a way of life; a vehicle for individuals to acquire economic freedom. It may take a revolution for people to gain their political freedom, but it only needs an individual's effort through entrepreneurial initiative to obtain economic freedom. Nonetheless, there is a fundamental question that has to be addressed: Can there be political freedom before economic freedom?

Entrepreneurship or Entrepreneur: That is the Question

The word "entrepreneurship" originated from the French word *entrepreneuriat* meaning "to undertake". In the nineteenth century, entrepreneurship was used to describe the new phenomenon of the individual who had come up with a venture idea, incubated it, assembled resources and created the new venture. For some strange reason, the process disappeared from early (approximately from 1700 to 1803) classical economics literature. The spirit of entrepreneurship was in limbo, until a soul catcher, Jean Baptiste Say, caught the soul and gave it a body. The entrepreneur as he perceived it, was a coordinator and supervisor in the production process, and the fourth agent (the other three are land, labour and capital) of the factors of production. Since then, everyone has jumped onto the bandwagon and begun to search for this creature's soul. But the search led to some important questions: How does it look? How does it behave? Collectively, what are its attributes and common characteristics?

Scholars and laymen alike, through research, observation, and/or simply listening to fairy tales, have made the entrepreneur look like a giant, say, with three eyes (two at the front, one in the back), four arms (two arms and hands counting money, the other two doing business), or four legs running faster than the TVG (a French commuter train that can travel at a speed of 350 kilometres per hour). It may have an X-ray eye, or perhaps it can go back to see the past or go forward into the future, like a crystal ball. Unfortunately, none of these is true. An entrepreneur is just another person.

Since we cannot find any visible difference physically between entrepreneurs and non-entrepreneurs, people started the soul-searching process to find what makes them tick, what their attributes are, and how they behave differently from others. The following three commonly acknowledged attributes are the result of an extensive soul-searching effort.

An Entrepreneur is a Moderate or Calculated Risk-taker

We say that an entrepreneur is a person who undertakes risks in the business world. My goodness, in this life who does not take risks? We risk coming into this world, we risk getting married and having children, and we even risk crossing the road. However, there is a difference between taking the risk of crossing the road and taking the risk of going into business. In crossing the road, you are risking your life; you might be run over by a car or perhaps by a herd of cattle if you are in Costa Rica. By going into business, the risk could be business failure and financial loss. To the Chinese, this would mean loss of face; to others, it might even result in suicide; there are also others who view business failure as another opportunity to make money. If your business is successful, you are an entrepreneur, but if you are unsuccessful, you are only an average Joe or Mary and nothing else, even though you have risked everything you have. You failed. Oh yes, you are a gambler, but not an entrepreneur. Does this remind you of soldiers in war? Often the only difference between a hero and a fool is who managed to dodge the last bullet.

Entrepreneurs have a High Need for Achievement

A high need for achievement has been identified by our behavioural scientists as one of the attributes for our beloved entrepreneurs. Can anybody honestly say he has no high need for achievement? The monk from a Buddist temple who finds life to be nothing but emptiness and submits himself to the rigorous ascetic discipline also has a high need for achievement, because he wants to be a buddha himself, the highest of all spiritual achievements. A high need for achievement is an embedded need for every individual. Children want to grow to be adults, because in their minds, adults can do everything that the children cannot do (such as staying up late, drinking, going to parties and coming home after midnight, etc.). A researcher may use the word "entrepreneurship" to develop a dissertation to earn a PhD degree; a teacher can use the word "entrepreneurship" and devote a lecture to it; a professor can use the same word to write a book and a dean of the "B" school can make it a lifetime career. All of these endeavours involve a need for some form of achievement; what is so different with the entrepreneur's high need for achievement? The only difference is the type of need.

Entrepreneurs have a High Need for Autonomy

Everyone in this country wants to be left alone, from children who have just started to talk to the politicians who run a country. Some years ago, the author was invited to give a guest lecture in a country which was under Canada's CIDA (Canadian International Development Agency) aid programme. At the opening ceremony of the lecture series, the Canadian high commissioner (ambassador) sitting next to me whispered in my ear: "Raymond, I don't know what I am here for. What I gather from the government here is: 'give us the money and leave us alone'." Autonomy is what makes us individuals, but what difference is there with respect to the high need for autonomy of our entrepreneurs?

In addition to the three attributes noted above, there are also at least a dozen more attributes described by someone and followed by a large number of others, as being identifiable attributes possessed by entrepreneurs. Today, if one is interested to look through all those attributes identified by people since 1803 and Jean Baptiste Say, to our present day nearly two centuries later, the whole thing is just like playing a broken record and hearing the same song over and over again. Only Schumpeter really made sense; he identified the creative and innovative attributes of entrepreneurs. On the other hand, we are all creative by birth, except that some people are more creative and innovative than others.

The Parade of "Entrepreneur" Definitions

In academics, the search for who said what is called a literature review. Doing a literature review of the word "entrepreneur" is like searching for the origins of little Red Riding Hood; it has numerous origins. Anyway, everything must have a starting point. Let us start with the following.

Richard Cantillon (1730), an economist in the early eighteenth century, described an entrepreneur as any individual who operates an undertaking under conditions where expenditures are known and certain, but incomes are unknown and uncertain. The uncertainty of income is due to the fact that the future market demand is not predictable. This individual was an entrepreneur in all but name. So, he said, an entrepreneur needs to have the foresight and willingness to assume risks and take the necessary action to seize profitable opportunities in the marketplace.

Jean-Baptiste Say (1803) described an entrepreneur as a coordinator and supervisor of production. He described an entrepreneur as a person who must have judgement, perseverance and a knowledge of the world as well as of business. He is required to estimate with tolerable accuracy, the importance of a specific product, and the probable demand and the means of its production. He must employ staff and/or labour, is responsible for procurement and must find the right market and constantly focus his attention on market movements both at home and worldwide.

Cantillon and Say were both economists. Behavioural scientists also have perceptions about entrepreneurs and we should examine those as well. D.C. McClelland (1961), a highly regarded behavioural scientist since the 1960s, pulled the entrepreneur away from the economists, and described entrepreneurs as individuals in need of high achievement. According to his theory, an entrepreneur is:

- responsible for solving problems, setting goals and reaching these goals through his own efforts;
- a moderate risk-taker, who takes risks based on his skills;
- knowledgeable of the results of the decision making and task accomplishment processes.

To McClelland, entrepreneurs are self-starters who appear to others to be internally driven by a strong desire to compete, to excel against self-imposed standards, and to pursue and attain challenging goals.

Writers expressing their views about what an entrepreneur should be need not limit themselves to these three, as there are many others who describe an entrepreneur with other qualities. Entrepreneurs have been variously described as organizers of resources, administrators of enterprise, geniuses in planning, and possessors of skills in communication, networking, negotiation and identifying market niches.

While people like Cantillon and Say gave their opinion as to what an entrepreneur should be, there are others who want to tell the world who an entrepreneur is. This time, let us go back to the 1960s.

There were two economists who attempted to define an entrepreneur almost simultaneously. Rotter (1961) described an entrepreneur as a person with an internal locus of control. This means that entrepreneurs believe in themselves and fate does not control their destiny. They believe that whatever they do, success or failure are under their control. Schumpeter (1971) perceived entrepreneurs to be innovators; they are born and not made, and they disturb the economic status quo through innovation. Schumpeter was very specific both about what an entrepreneur is and what an entrepreneur is not. According to him:

1. Entrepreneurs are not necessarily capitalists.
2. Entrepreneurs need not be inventors.
3. Entrepreneurs are not necessarily managers.
4. Entrepreneurs cannot always be associated with a particular group of individuals (for example, business persons).
5. Entrepreneurs are social deviants.

It seems that to define an entrepreneur is such a fun exercise for academics; everyone of them has their five cents worth to offer. These include Baumback (1981) and Welsh and White (1983), who describe an impressive eleven characteristics of an entrepreneur: good health (I am sure, everyone should be in good health), realism, superior conceptual ability, self-confidence, a need to control or direct (internal locus of control), attraction to challenges, sufficient emotional stability, self-control, initiative, balance and control and enterprise (self-reliant attitude supported by confidence in one's ability to take risks).

The Parade

Having had a taste of what academics do to the poor general public, and if in any event you have the desire to know more, here is a partial parade of their ideas.

Summary of definitions of an entrepreneur

The list in Table 5.1 is by no means complete, but it should give us a very good idea of how we have struggled for more than two centuries just to find out who an entrepreneur is.

Table 5.1
Summary of definitions of an entrepreneur

Contributors	Period	Contribution
Richard Cantillon	1730	A self-employed person with uncertain returns
Abbe Nicollas	1767	A leader of men, a manager of resources, an innovator of ideas, including new scientific ideas, and a risk-taker
Jean-Baptiste Say	1803/1810	A coordinator of production with managerial talent
Joseph Schumpeter	1910	A creative innovator
Frank Knight	1921	A manager responsible for direction and control, who bears uncertainty
Edith Penrose	1959	A person with managerial capabilities separate from entrepreneurial capabilities, and able to identify opportunities and develop small enterprises
J. E. Stepanek	1960	A moderate risk-taker
D. C. McClelland	1961	A person with a high need for achievement
Robert L. Budner	1962	A person with a high tolerance for ambiguity
Orvis F. Collins	1964	A person with a high need for autonomy
W. D. Litzinger	1965	Low need for support and conformity, leadership, decisiveness, determination, perseverance and integrity
J. B. Rotter	1976	Internal locus of control
Israel Kirzner	1979	An arbitrageur
J. A. Timmons	1985	"A" type bahaviour pattern

There are dozens of others who have said the same or similar things about the entrepreneur, including Hornaday (1971), Bosley (1980), Kogan (1964), Sexton (1985), Roberts (1968), Bunker (1970), Bowman (1983) and many others who wrote at different times or to different audiences.

Back home in Canada, after having gone through the list with my MBA students, one student said to me that this was purely an academic exercise. I agreed with her, but I said it was more than an academic exercise, it was also torture.

A comparison between the works of Hornaday and Gibb

If the preceding list is a bit lengthy, it might be useful to have a summary of summaries. For this, we are grateful to J. A. Hornaday and Allan A. Gibb who provided separate summaries of these ideas outlined in Table 5.2.

Table 5.2
A comparison between the works of Hornaday and Gibb

Hornaday*	Gibb**
Self-confidence	Creativity
Perseverance, determination	Initiative
Energy, diligence	High achievement
Resourcefulness	Risk-taking (moderate)
Ability to take calculated risks	Leadership
Need to achieve	Autonomy and independence
Creativity	Analytical ability
Initiative	Hard work
Flexibility	Good communication skills
Independence	
Foresight	
Dynamism, leadership	
Ability to get along with people and criticism	
Profit-orientation	
Perceptiveness	
Optimism	

Sources: *In Pleitner (1986); **Gibb (1986/87).

This comparison shows us that many people think about who an entrepreneur is, but it is not difficult to realize that not one single definition mentions anything relating the entrepreneur with society. It is no wonder even people involved in organized crime consider themselves as entrepreneurs, especially if they have the same attributes as described above by some of the contributors.

The Frustration: Can You be Henry Ford, Chew Choo Keng or Mary Kay Ash?

Some successful entrepreneurs have become legendary folk heroes. Researchers and academics have studied them, and the general public wants to emulate them. I suppose there is something to this if entrepreneurs are really successful individuals with money, power, connections and are saviours of the market economy. So writing about how to become a successful entrepreneur has become an enterprise itself. Educators, journalists, politicians and celebrities have all indulged in this game to some extent. Though they speak in different ways, they all, in some way, use entrepreneurial attributes to their rescue. It appears that if a person has the same attributes as a publicly noted entrepreneur, it is sufficient to consider him as an entrepreneur. Unfortunately (or should I say, fortunately) every person is unique. Besides, to be successful, you also need the opportunity, the environment and, among other things, the resources. By recognizing the environment, the opportunity and what we know as the "visional desired outcome", and if you could continuously apply your creative thoughts, you may become a successful entrepreneur (by your own standard and definition of success). But you can never be Henry Ford, Chew Choo Keng or Mary Kay Ash. In order to be a successful entrepreneur, your attributes and proper application of these attributes can only account for 50 per cent of the total score; for the other 50 per cent you can do little more than get down on your knees and pray for God's help. The success stories of Henry Ford, Chew Choo Keng or Mary Kay Ash can only serve as a motivating factor: If they can do it, why can't I? The bottom line is that there are millions or perhaps billions of individuals with the same attributes as those successful entrepreneurs. They behave, make decisions, and act as entrepreneurs and they are entrepreneurs, but only the successful ones (particularly, financially successful) get noticed.

There is one more source of frustration which is seldom recognized in public, but which was impressed upon me by one of my MBA students (Wee Hui Kan) at the Nanyang Technological University of Singapore. He argued that if you are an entrepreneur with a wonderful idea but did not bring the idea successfully to the market, your creative contribution will not be recognized, so you are not an entrepreneur. But if someone copies your idea and brings about a successful business venture, he will be credited with the success and creativity, and he is an entrepreneur. It is the person who gets it to work in the marketplace who counts, not so much the one who thought of the idea. In contrast, in the field of scientific discovery, there is great significance in being the first one to come up with an idea because the discovery of the idea is the end itself.

The value to the individual of knowing the entrepreneur's attributes at the most, is to improve self-awareness or perhaps self-assessment. What is important is not merely knowing the attributes, but seeing how these attributes relate to decision making behaviour and transform them into actions where actions are required. For this reason, prior to the publication of the works of Gibb and Pleitner, I joined approximately ninety of my students in a group project, to attempt to test those entrepreneur's attributes advanced by various individuals, such as good communication skills, flexibility, risk-taking, positive response to changes, dynamism, and optimism. We contacted, informally interviewed, and observed approximately ninety owner/managers of entrepreneurial under-takings, fifty managers of large corporations and several administrators of three post-secondary educational institutions (I considered them to be similar to managers of large corporations). We then discussed their different management practices and decision making behaviour, to find out whether their actions and decision making behaviour were in congruence with those attributes advanced by various researchers. The findings, in general, agreed with those attributes (or characteristics) described in Table 5.2 earlier. Moreover, as a by-product, we also found there were large discrepancies in business practices and decision making behaviour between those who manage their own businesses (the entrepreneurs) and those who manage someone else's businesses (large corporations and educational institutions). For illustration purpose, the findings were grouped into two categories: entrepreneurial behaviour and management practices, and corporate or institutional managerial behaviour and practices (see Table 5.3).

In addition, the findings among researchers also reveal at least one transparent difference between entrepreneurs and corporate and institutional managers: concern for equity or ownership. Whilst in an entrepreneur-managed firm, the words "my business" are used, "our company (or "the company"/"the institution") is used by managers working as employees of large corporations. It should also be clear that entrepreneurs are action-oriented individuals; if there is no action, there is no entrepreneurship.

Table 5.3
Summary of the findings on entrepreneur's attributes

	Entrepreneurial behaviour and management practices	Corporate or institutional managerial behaviour and practices
Basic difference	Owner-managed firms	Large corporations and educational institutions
Principals	Entrepreneurs	Managers and administrators
Performance	Judged in the marketplace	Judged by superiors
Management style	Hands on, personal attention and "homemade" procedures along with personalized management	Delegation, the use of control systems, procedures and manuals
Business objective	Identical to the entrepreneur's personal objective. For example, self-employment, to provide jobs to family members, to realize a dream, to control his own destiny and/or to be rich and famous	Rate of return to investors or meeting the budgetary requirements in the case of administrator
Profit	A residual to the entrepreneur	Earnings to the corporation
Attitude to new tasks	There are perceived opportunities in every problem situation. More in identifying and pursuing opportunities	Every opportunity has conceived problems. More in problem solving
Attitude toward the presence of an opportunity	Let us do what we can to make it happen	Do a cost and benefit analysis
Attitude toward risks	If the risk is too great, find alternatives, otherwise, risk is a challenge	Risk is to be avoided, otherwise, attempts to be made to reduce, or eliminate the risk
Attitude towards making a decision	Make the decision and take the consequences	Sound out ideas to a few more people, or better still, call a meeting, form a task force, a committee and/ or do a study

Table 5.3 (cont'd)

	Entrepreneurial behaviour and management practices	Corporate or institutional managerial behaviour and practices
Decision making behaviour	Try it out first, and see what happens. If necessary, smooth out the rough spots	Seek out perfect information
Deal with crisis	Put out fire first: a fire fighter's approach	Let's find out who is responsible: an investigator's approach
Action orientation	Do it now before it is too late	Opportunities are like buses, they come and they go. Just as there is always another bus, there are always more opportunities
The process of management	Based on the business growth cycle (i.e. incubation, start-up, development, growth)	Based on business functions (i.e. marketing, production, finance)
Attitude toward customers	Maintain close relations with customers	Have someone else to look after them, as there are more important things to do
Communication	Verbal, person to person, if possible. Answer every telephone call personally, otherwise, take number and call back later, normally within 24 hours	Secretary screens incoming phone calls. Often only "VIPs" get through, otherwise, the caller is told to leave a message, which may or may not be returned

The Parade of Definitions of Entrepreneurship

As academicians tend to make life uneasy for others, they make their own lives miserable as well. To define who an entrepreneur is and what entrepreneurship is are the cases in point. The truth of the matter is, some academicians never seem to trouble themselves to differentiate between what entrepreneurship is and who an entrepreneur is. There are many who made great efforts to define who an entrepreneur is but got it mixed up with entrepreneurship as well. While we pursue the definition of who an entrepreneur is, because we wish to find out what entrepreneurship is, nevertheless, they are not the same. It is entrepreneurship that we can use to apply to our endeavours, but not to duplicate other people's attributes. Unfortunately, economists and behavioural scientists have devoted much effort to the definition of "entrepreneur", but the same is not true for "entrepreneurship". Some of the more noted efforts are outlined in Table 5.4.

Table 5.4
Summary of entrepreneurship definitions

Contributor	Period	Contribution
Carl Menger	1871	Entrepreneurship involves: obtaining information, calculation, an act of will and supervision
Joseph Schumpeter	1910	Entrepreneurship is in its essence the finding and promoting of new combination of productive factors
Harvey Leibenstein	1970	Entrepreneurship is the reduction of organizational inefficiency and the reversal of organizational entropy
Israel Kirzner	1975	The identification of market arbitrage opportunities
W. Ed McMullan and Wayne A. Long	1990	Entrepreneurship is the building of new growth organizations
Howard H. Stevenson	1992*	Entrepreneurship is the pursuit of opportunity beyond the resources currently under your control

* Noted from a public lecture given by Professor Stevenson in Singapore (1992). The author assumes the responsibility for its accuracy.

Intrepreneurship: Why It Failed its Blood Test

Entrepreneurship is recognized as wealth creation and a value adding process (see page 83). Its dynamism also attracted a great deal of attention from those responsible for the managing of large corporations. As noted from Table 5.3, although limited by the sample size, corporate management is hindered by corporate culture. The root of this is no less than organizational failure. People become isolated from the organization, then from each other as the organization grows in size. The following illustration is a case in point.

Organization Overload

Assumptions:

1. Corporate expansion makes it necessary to expand operations through the restructuring of the organization, or in other words, through playing with organization charts.
2. Through the restructuring, tasks are delegated, functions are divided and responsibilities are assigned.
3. In most cases, divisional structure allows divisional autonomy.
4. While operations can be divisionalized in order not to lose corporate control, it is necessary to expand staff functions and increase the "controlling" power of the functional staff.
5. A rigid management control system is established, specifying a formal reporting system to clearly identify responsibility and operational authority.
6. Tasks are delegated, if the task
   (a) can be performed independently by an individual;
   (b) is of a routine nature;
   (c) has results which are measurable by some form of management control system;
   (d) is within the scope of the general direction of the corporate strategy;
   (e) does not require significant discretional decisions;
   (f) is within the scope of performance of competent managers.

On the basis of the preceding assumptions, an organization can be overloaded with layers and layers of reporting (see Figure 5.1). Under the circumstances, the isolation of people from the organization seems to be a rule rather than an exception.

In some organizations, the layers of the reporting process could be as thick as a roll of bathroom tissue. In order for a subordinate to reach a superior, such as a small department manager who wishes to speak to the general manager, he would probably have to go through as many as five steps, and even at the last step he could be stopped by the personal assistant saying: "I am sorry, GM is at a meeting." (See Figure 5.2.)

I admit that I may be guilty of a little exaggeration, but anyone who wishes to reach a corporate executive or anyone in a position of power could easily experience that terrible sound of music many times over, before you finally reach the real person.

The illustration attempts to show one thing: as an organization grows in size, more often than not, it becomes convenient to separate the people from the organization, and further separate people from

Figure 5.1
A chart for organization overload

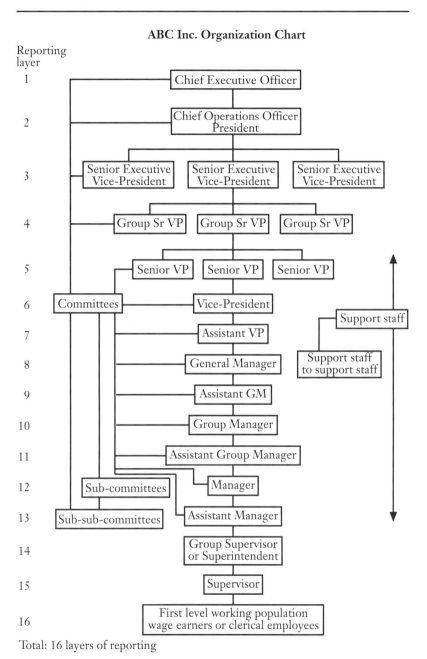

ABC Inc. Organization Chart

Figure 5.2
Inter-departmental communication: "I am sorry, Mr Big is at a meeting"

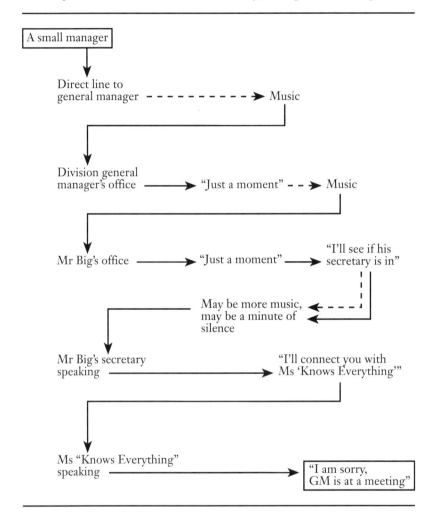

themselves as well. When in isolation, individuals tend to be more protective and defensive, and when everything seems to be thrown into the unknown, the practice of management by fear will come as an inevitable consequence.

Management by Fear

As the organization becomes bigger and bigger, individuals tend to play with the organization chart, issue memos, chase paper and lose contact with their colleagues and their superiors. Therefore, it is not difficult to find a lack of employee commitment to the corporate goal, and to some extent even to their own work. The nine-to-five routine becomes a reality, and no one is willing to make any discretionary decisions.

As the organization evolves, it becomes increasingly difficult to have superiors close to their subordinates and as people lose contact with each other, the old concept of management by objective can turn into management by exception, reinforced by management control systems mostly designed by non-line experience functional experts. Eventually this becomes management by fear. Once the corporate culture becomes the practice of management by fear, individuals will learn soon enough and practise defensive management to protect their own skins. There will be no initiative, no feeling of the common good (not even decency), and more often than not, some individuals in the organization will use other people's efforts to add to their personal credit, blame others for their wrong decisions and wrong actions and will deny everything if there is any irregularity detected.

In some organizations, attempts have been made to initiate incentive systems. The result is not difficult to predict. The incentive systems only make people commit to the incentive, which is only a secondary factor of motivation. At best, incentive systems function as a positive reinforcement toward tasks well done, but do nothing for the primary motive of identification with the organization. At worst, it lowers the standard of performance (no incentive, no efforts), and is an open admission of failure in management.

Entrepreneurship Definition Comes to the Rescue

Out of desperation, the search for alternatives began, and after a period of puzzling, it was found that entrepreneurship was the logical choice.

> Entrepreneurship is the attempt to create value through recognition of business opportunity, the management of risk-taking appropriate to the opportunity, and through communicative and management skills to mobilize human, financial, and material resources necessary to bring a project to fruition.

This fits in well with what corporate executives want, for without losing a cent, the idea of being entrepreneurial can really stimulate people to resuscitate the "wounded" organization. However, it will not be appropriate to call it corporate entrepreneurship since there is the ownership problem. Therefore, a new word was added to the dictionary:

intrepreneurship. Why not? Just by introducing the term intrepreneurship is a creative endeavour in itself.

What is intrepreneurship? In essence, it is a corporate effort attempting to revitalize the individual's efforts by incorporating some entrepreneurial concepts into the corporate culture:

1. Award ownership of new ideas to the individual who developed the idea.
2. Give operational freedom to the operational person to perform the tasks.
3. Reinforce the corporate culture (whatever it may be).
4. Encourage small team interactions in the organization.
5. Promote individuals to identify themselves with the team as well as the organization.
6. Encourage individuals to develop a postitive attitude.

There are some other measures but those listed above are the essentials.

This can seem very exciting when you look at the old horse of corporate culture. By marrying it to the young filly, entrepreneurship, one hopes to breathe new life into the old boy. But closer examination reveals that you cannot solve real problems by saying a prayer and you cannot save corporate culture by defining a new word. In short, intrepreneurship failed its blood test.

To award ownership of new ideas creates a problem to accountants, because they have not been trained to determine the value of a new idea, and they do not know what to do with the opportunity cost. The third and fifth points are a rehash of old management gimmicks and the last point on intrepreneurship is just words without any substance. Only the second point seems to make some sense but it is also nothing to be excited about, since some twenty, perhaps thirty years ago, the idea of organizing corporations into various centres, mainly cost centres and profit centres had already been conceived.

A profit centre is defined as a centre having the following characteristics:

- Operational independence
- Revenue and cost separately accounted for
- A manager is responsible for the profit performance of the centre
- Managers can freely negotiate transfer pricing among division managers for divisional goods and services transfers

There is little difference between this definition and an application of intrepreneurship in reality.

What we have failed to understand is that entrepreneurship is built on ownership or equity (blood, sweat, passion and love). Without a commitment on equity from individuals of the organization, intrepreneurship cannot work. It cannot pass its blood test because it has no blood.

What is to follow? Frankly, I do not know. Perhaps corporate decision makers should also search their souls, and ask these questions:

1. What is the purpose of life?
2. What is the purpose of being a corporation?
3. What is the purpose of wanting to be big and having plenty, after all, once the real person is dead, all he needs at most is a three square metre plot, or a jar?
4. Do we want to take everything, including our children into the three square metre plot, or do we want them to live and enjoy life as we did?

What is Entrepreneurship and Who is an Entrepreneur?

Geography tells us that as human beings, we have only two choices: we can either change the environment to suit our needs, or change ourselves to fit into the environment. As we are essentially energy, we have a tendency to try to change ourselves to fit into the environment, and once we get familiar with the environment, we will then change the environment to suit our needs. Some people can go far with this philosophy — they run their lives in accordance with their desires, if not all the time, then most of the time.

We want to fit entrepreneurship within our own terms and hence, drug traffickers, criminal bosses, people in business who deliberately harm others for financial gains, and people exploiting the earth just for the sake of making a profit with no consideration for the future, consider themselves to be entrepreneurs. One Hong Kong newspaper even gives the criminals the glorious title: criminal entrepreneurs.

What troubles me the most is that in the past 250 years, other than Cantillon (1730) and Edith Penrose (1959) who made direct references to entrepreneurs as business persons, no one else limited entrepreneurs to business undertakings. As for entrepreneurship, only Kirzner (1973) noted the word "market" in his contribution, and during the last two decades, everyone who's thinking, writing, talking about entrepreneurship seems to exclusively associate it with business undertakings. Is this a true perspective of our society, or is it a convenience to suit our needs?

There are clear indications that entrepreneurship is the process of creating wealth, and entrepreneurs are individuals involved in the creation of wealth. There is never any direct reference to society, as if society does not exist, and humanity is nothing but just after-dinner talk. No wonder we have *Time*'s headline "All God's creations priced to sell" (*Time*, 19 July 1993), and "Japanese fishermen ignore the international ban on whale hunting" (Singapore Broadcasting Corporation News, 10 November 1993). Auto makers are almost aimlessly making and pushing increasing numbers of new cars to the market without any regard for the cost to the environment, just to accommodate their need for profit (of course, they will say for jobs as well). Some years ago, executives of a big auto maker, on account of the advice from the firm's attorney, decided to deal with individual lawsuits instead of recalling potentially lethally flawed cars on the basis of cost. Now, what does this say about our capitalist society?

Definitions are meaningless, unless they are used for application, in which case they affect decisions, shape people's thinking and guide individual actions. In this sense, definitions are important, and to define entrepreneurship and entrepreneur, we must have in mind that entrepreneurship functions in a framework within the environment, and entrepreneurs must act both in their interest and the interest of society. Therefore, entrepreneurship is not merely about business, it must be considered as an individual's attitude, and a way of life. There are not many people who can deny that we must create wealth and add value. The wealth creating and value-adding responsibility is not just for business persons, but for every single individual on earth. Therefore, the following definitions were offered:

- **Entrepreneurship** is the *process* of doing something new (creative) and something different (innovative) for the purpose of creating wealth for the individual and adding value to society.

- An **entrepreneur** is a *person* who undertakes a wealth-creating and value-adding process, through incubating ideas, assembling resources and making things happen (Kao, 1993).

- **Enterprising culture** is a *commitment* of the individual to the continuing pursuit of opportunities and developing an entrepreneurial endeavour to its growth potentials for the purpose of creating wealth for the individual and adding value to society.

Appendix 5.1

The Creation of Wealth and Value — Yet Another Definition of Entrepreneurship

Wee-Liang Tan

It seems strange that we should in this journal be defining entrepreneurship as if it were a philosophy in Raymond W. Y. Kao's definitions that emblazons the inside cover of the journal. They are unlike other definitions of entrepreneurship that have focused either on the individual entrepreneur, his or her traits, or a process that ranges from the pre-launch to post-launch stages of a business venture. One might argue that it does not provide a working definition for research in view of its breadth.

However, if one were to be open-minded, not dismiss the definitions and examine them, one discovers that they do provide a liberating and all encompassing idea — they supply meaning and purpose to those who seek to put them into practice. The definitions can only be practised if there is the accompanying attitude changes: wealth creation, value creation and the creation of these in the context of self and not self alone but the world. These attitude changes are the essence of the definitions. It is a liberating set of definitions for they expand the boundaries of entrepreneurship. Entrepreneurship is for everyone who seeks to practise wealth and value creation. It can feature in an individual who is an employee or in a firm where the enterprising culture exists. One is not required to be the founder-owner of new ventures.

The cynics at this stage would say that all these are balderdash — entrepreneurship should not be defined in such an all-embracing manner. However, the cynics should be reminded that no other definition has received universal acceptance for one reason or another. One possible reason for the rejection of previous definitions has been their perceived incompleteness.

Of Kao's definitions, on the other hand, one cannot say the same. Perhaps the reason entrepreneurship has defied an easy definition since its early days lies in the fact that the earlier definitions failed to accommodate other individuals, other than business founders or the managerial risk-takers.

Relevance of the New Definitions

Entrepreneurship, thus defined, is very relevant today when it is tempting in the light of the democratic revolution (Greshman, C., 1989), to think that a mere change of a political system (from communism to democracy) or a change in the economic system from a command economy to a market system will automatically translate into a change in a country's economic prospects for prosperity. It would be a gross error to think that now with most nations, if not every nation, formerly aligned with communism deciding to "Go West", that this would signal greater prosperity for the former communist countries making the switch to democracy.

It is true that democracy has rebounded from its perceived fate in the 1970s when Senator Patrick Moynihan observed that liberal democracy "is where the world was not where it is going ..." Increasingly, democracy is seen as an arrangement peculiar to a handful of North Atlantic countries (Moynihan, D. P., 1975). However, the introduction of democracy in itself does not guarantee anything. An eminent MIT political scientist Brad Roberts noted that "As a generator of short-term bursts of high growth rates or of the rapid redistribution of wealth, democracies have not always done as well as a few — or badly as most — authoritarian states. Over the long run, however, democracies tend to promote the steady accumulation and distribution of national wealth at a pace that does not tear apart the social fabric" (Roberts, B., 1990). Democracy does not guarantee growth. Worse still, it could be democracy only in name. After all, it has been observed that even dictators have been known to use the language of democracy to lend legitimacy to their causes (Dahl, R. A., 1989).

A change in the economic system, too, does not always lead to economic success. There are numerous examples of late that illustrate this. Russia and the former East Germany still possess economic woes. Britain, a nation that has a market economy and contributed some of the leading economic minds, including Adam Smith, T. R. Malthus, J. S. Mill, J. M. Keynes and J. R. Hicks, has an economy known for its slow growth (Olson, M., 1990).

More is required than just a democratic political system or a market economy. How else can one explain why another Marshall Plan may not work today in another nation though it once worked in post-war Germany (Dahrendorf, F., 1987)? It could be as Dahrendorf observed as a need for motivation — "What values are peculiarly suited or unsuited to get modern economies going?" — and a removal of the obstacles to participation in the economic process (Dahrendorf, F., 1987). He added that "[a] modern economy cannot rely on passive participation alone. In one form or another, Joseph Schumpeter's entrepreneurs have to be added to Keynes' measures to stimulate demand." If Kao's definitions had been available earlier, he could have referred to "Kao's" entrepreneurs.

Entrepreneurship as defined by Raymond Kao permits every individual to participate in all aspects of life, to contribute to wealth and value in its broadest sense, for self and always for society. Thus defined, entrepreneurship has much in common with democracy in its original form — the Greek democratic city-state. In the city-state then, according to Robert Dahl, in "the Greek vision of democracy, the citizen is a whole person for whom politics is a natural social activity not sharply separated from the rest of life...." (Dahl, R. A., 1989). Every citizen participated in the government of the state at assemblies and in holding office. It is in the democratic idea of participation that Raymond's definition of entrepreneurship for everyone has in common: through entrepreneurship everyone can participate not only economically but also socially. Modern democracy is the original concept of democracy transformed to accommodate the large number of people in a nation-state as opposed to a city-state (Dahl, R. A., 1989).

There may be forces in a modern democracy that "seem to conspire against innovation and initiative" (Dahrendorf, F., 1987). However, one hopes that Kao's ideas about entrepreneurship will bring about change. The definitions are timely because in this day and age, the individual often thinks that entrepreneurship is only for the select few with the flair and capacity for risk-taking. If the individual were an employee, he or she would leave matters to others, relegating his or her role to that minimum required by management. It is entrepreneurship by individuals, whether individually or collectively, that leads to the growth potential of the various economies within which they reside. They account not only for the new combinations described by Schumpeter, the corporate giants, but also for the higher productivity that speaks for national economic well-being.

References

Dahl, R.A. (1989). *Democracy and Its Critics*. New Haven: Yale University Press, 18.

Dahrendorf, F. (1987). Adam Smith was an optimist. *The Washington Quarterly* 10 (4).

Greshman, C. (1989). The United States and the world democractic revolution. *The Washington Quarterly* 12 (1).

Moynihan, D.P. (1975). The American Experiment. *The Public Interest* Fall 6–7.

Olson, M. (1990). Is Britain the wave of the future? How ideas affect societies. In Mann, M. (ed.). *The Rise and Decline of the Nation State*. Oxford, U.K. and Cambridge, Massachusetts: Basil Blackwell.

Roberts, B. (1990). *The New Democracies: Global Change and U.S. Policy*. Cambridge, Massachusetts: The MIT Press.

Source: Editorial, *Journal of Enterprising Culture*, Vol. 1, Nos 3 and 4, 1994.

Appendix 5.2

From General Management to Entrepreneurship: The Business ("B") School Challenge

Raymond W. Y. Kao

The "B" School

Today, virtually every university in the world has a business ("B") school, school of management, or faculty of management that provides business-management education leading to the degree of Master of Business Administration (MBA) or its equivalent.

Historically, it was the Pennsylvania University which, in the early part of this century, created the first "B" school, Wharton School of Business, paving the way for further development of "B" schools in universities as we know it today. The objective of the Wharton School, at the time, was to train rich, younger generations for the purpose of taking care of their family businesses. "B" schools today have been developed to be higher learning institutions designed to some extent for individuals to manage other people's business.

The General-Management Model, and the Imbalance of the "B" School Curriculum

In responding to the market need, a large number of "B" schools evolved from developing individuals to becoming applied generalists (general management) to specialists in their respective disciplines, such as marketing and accounting, with the general approach to MBA education still within the framework of general management, a model derived from assuming management to be separated from ownership. Under the general-management model, management is a profession governed by professional training to manage business entities in the interests of their shareholders. In particular, the attentions of managers and of multinational corporations, who rely heavily on raising capital from the public, more often than not are directed to the movement of the corporation's share price traded in the stock market.

The general-management model provided a good base for "B" school success for decades. However, the idea of developing individuals to manage other people's businesses was questioned by many concerned individuals and organizations. In the 1970s, lobbyists such as the National

Federation of Independent Business (USA) and Canadian Federation of Independent Business openly criticized the "B" schools for not responding to the societal need to develop small firms (or independent businesses) which were the sources of employment, particularly new jobs. Universities were not entirely ignorant of the need for small-business management. Since as far back as in the 1930s, Kobe University introduced an "entrepreneurship" course and Grant Moon inaugurated a similar course in small-business management or entrepreneurship at the University of South Dakota in 1954. By the 1970s, courses and programs in small-business management and entrepreneurship were, in fact, mushrooming from coast to coast in the US and Canada. In the early 1980s, the International Council for Small Business (ICSB), based in the US, was able to collect course information about small-business management, entrepreneurship and new-venture management from more than 500 universities and colleges.

The author had the opportunity to examine these small business/ entrepreneurship course syllabuses from information collected by ICSB and similar information from the Canadian source. It was found that, even though there were noted differences reflected in the element of hands-on management style in the earlier venture start-up and early stages of development, subject contents, course structure, methods of instruction and course requirements were governed basically by the general-management model — a management framework that assumed management to be a profession separated from business ownership.

From Small-Business Management to Entrepreneurship

Although entrepreneurship may be defined differently from small business, there was a general tendency to assume that entrepreneurship was directly associated with profit-making business undertakings, particularly the creation of small enterprises. This is not difficult to comprehend, since the creation and development of a small business is, in fact, a wealth-creation process, an entrepreneurial endeavour by its own right. The development of small businesses at least during the 1970s and 1980s was very much the focus of efforts not only in "B" schools, but also in the marketplace.

In the early 1980s, there was a shift in emphasis. Rather than focusing on developing small businesses for the sake of creating jobs, the paradigm shifted to the development of entrepreneurship in the interest of creating wealth. In particular, since the downfall of the Soviet Union, and the deep recession experienced by "capitalist" countries, entrepreneurship seems to have earned its place as the obvious solution to the two extreme ideologies: socialism on one hand and capitalism on the other.

As it stands, the whole world seems to have elevated itself to a new order: to develop entrepreneurship in the interest of the economy and the nation's prosperity, not necessary for "wealth creation" alone, but also to encourage individuals to be self-reliant and shift away from government reliance. The emergence of the new wave of entrepreneurship has also prompted university "B" schools to take the initiative of introducing entrepreneurship into the curriculum at a much faster pace than in the 1970s and early 1980s. This new development also brought along new challenges, most of them built around the issue of whether or not entrepreneurship should be an academic discipline in higher learning institutions.

Should Entrepreneurship be an Independent Academic Discipline?

There are pros and cons as to whether or not entrepreneurship should be an independent academic discipline. They can be summarized:

1. The "yes" group
   a. Entrepreneurship has a distinct role in the wealth-creation process.
   b. Entrepreneurship contains a distinct body of knowledge, and distinct process including methods, concepts and theories used in inquiries.
   c. Two perceptions on entrepreneurship, the venture start-up position and the venture-growth position, cannot be included in a general-management framework which assumes business management to be distinct from business ownership.

2. The "no" group
   a. A great deal of "entrepreneurship" material overlaps with other courses. And any part of entrepreneurship can be included in other disciplines.
   b. Entrepreneurship cannot be taught. "B" schools are not the best environment for students to create new ventures. Why is an "entrepreneurship" subject/program necessary?
   c. "Entrepreneurship" is assumed to be having one's own business. To start one's own business does not require a great deal of advanced business management. But a course on small-business management will serve the same purpose. If, on the other hand, a smaller firm growing to be a large company, for example, reaches a sales volume greater than $50 million, it will require

professional management which will not be any different from other courses already offered in "B" schools.

Should entrepreneurship be an academic discipline in "B" schools? This is not the question; the real challenge is threefold:

1. Should entrepreneurship be associated with only profit-making business undertakings?
2. Should the teaching of business in "B" schools be primarily to develop individuals to work for other people's businesses and continue to be governed by the general-management model throughout "B" school?
3. Do academicians recognize the inadequacy within the general-management model in dealing with people problems in business, because the model is based primarily on the premise that management should be separate from ownership?

Should Entrepreneurship be Viewed as Only Profit-making Business Undertakings?

As Irvin Fisher, a noted US economist during the earlier years of this century, stressed, a good definition should be good for application, but the academic community seems to be unable to clearly define what entrepreneurship is and who an entrepreneur is. Subsequently, what the general public can grasp is that entrepreneurship is the process of profit-making through business undertakings, and an entrepreneur is the person who owns and manages the business for the purpose of making profits. There is nothing wrong with this perception except, if it holds true, then criminal activities for personal financial gains would be the practice of entrepreneurship, and persons who undertake criminal activities would be entrepreneurs, or criminal entrepreneurs as termed by a Hong Kong newspaper.

It is equally disturbing for people to see that entrepreneurship is exclusively associated with the creation of a new venture and the owning of one's own small business. However, both owning one's own business and the creation of a new venture are nevertheless entrepreneurship in practice, if there are creative and/or innovative activities in the endeavour. A small business owner/manager operating his/her own business without updating its operation and finding new and more meaningful innovative ways to better the firm's position (including maintaining its competitive position in the marketplace) will only be owner/manager of a small business, not necessary an entrepreneur.

For the purpose of furthering entrepreneurship development, so that it can be applied meaningfully to human endeavours, the author provides two definitions of entrepreneurship and entrepreneur:

> **ENTREPRENEURSHIP:** Entrepreneurship is "the process of doing something new (creative) and something different (innovative) for the purpose of creating wealth for the individual and adding value to society".
>
> **ENTREPRENEUR:** An entrepreneur is "a person who undertakes a wealth-creating and value-adding process, through incubating ideas, assembling resources and making things happen".
>
> Source: Raymond W.Y. Kao, Defining Entrepreneurship, Past, Present and ? *Creativity and Innovation Management*, Volume 2, No. 1, March 1993, Basil Blackwell Ltd., Oxford, 1993.

The provision in the definition has made it necessary for the inclusion of "wealth creating" and "value adding", but it should be noted that "wealth" means more than merely "profit" and/or "money". It could mean "financial", "knowledge" and/or "wisdom", whereas in "adding value", it is essential that activities harmful to other people or society and the environment should be excluded.

On the basis of these definitions, entrepreneurship is applicable to all economic endeavours; owning one's own business is only one of many human endeavours.

The General-Management Model and Entrepreneurship in "B" School Curriculum

The general-management model is built on the premise that to continue a firm's growth, professional management is required, but management is to be separated from ownership. Ownership is held by equity holders, and those working for the firm are employees of the company whose function is to ensure that resources under their trust are effectively and efficiently used to yield the maximum (or desirable) rate of return on the shareholders' investment. Even top-level executives/managers are employees. Therefore, if an entrepreneurship course/subject/program is introduced in "B" schools and continues to be dominated by the general-management model, it will be a misfit because of the fundamental difference in dealing with business ownership and business management. Under the circumstances, entrepreneurship is no more than another course in business management under the same assumption that the objective of the firm is to maximize (or optimize) shareholders' rate of return on their capital investment.

The General-Management Model and its Limitations

The model

The success of using general management to develop management strategies is not coincidental. It is like a triangle comprising the current accounting practice, the requirement set by the stock-exchange commission for corporate reporting on a worldwide basis and the general-management model. This makes it the strongest conceptual base to guide business management in recent decades.

The general-management model assumes that a corporation requires public financing to support its development and growth, and investors will invest in a particular corporation only if the rate of return on their investment is better than other options. The rate of return on investment, on the other hand, must be derived on the basis of the prescribed reporting standards, so the investors can rely on the report (through analysis) to make an intelligent investment decision. The function of the prescribed reporting standards is, of course, performed by professional accountants whose responsibility is to ensure that the reporting standards are maintained throughout the world. It should be clearly understood that investors are individuals with no means to act collectively (other than through their agents), but rely on the intermediary, the stock exchange, to exercise the necessary control through listing requirements and other means to enforce standards. In short, today, the management of a corporation is essentially governed by:

Figure 1
The general management and its inter-relationship with corporate financial reporting and stock exchange requirements

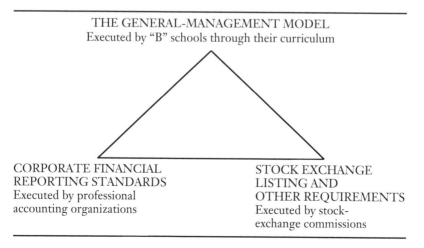

THE GENERAL-MANAGEMENT MODEL
Executed by "B" schools through their curriculum

CORPORATE FINANCIAL
REPORTING STANDARDS
Executed by professional
accounting organizations

STOCK EXCHANGE
LISTING AND
OTHER REQUIREMENTS
Executed by stock-
exchange commissions

The limitations

The general-management model has its limitations which are essentially rooted by its built-in assumption that management be separated from ownership, creating walls between those who work for a living and those who invest for financial gain. Consequently, it is not unusual to find corporate managers constantly engaged in a hopeless battle of motivating "unmotivatable employees". To overcome the difficulty, countless colleagues from the academic community have introduced countless concepts and programs such as vision sharing, team work, goal congruence, management by objective, incentive plans and a host of others. They have been proven useful and have been adopted by the business community for better management and they have also helped a large number of management consultants make a lot of money. Nevertheless, they tend to generate only short-term results, and are unable to cultivate, nurture and develop individuals' passion and love for the organization as a human-resources-based long-term organizational development and growth strategy.

Every concept or program has its merits. The tragedy is that general management recognizes "money" as the focal point of business management, whereas the creation of business, its development and growth, always rely on people and money. The equity of any organization consists always of those who invest their time, passion and love on one hand and those who invest money on the other. Corporate executives as well as colleagues in the academic community are aware of the importance of "entrepreneurship" in the organization; hence, they introduce the concept of "interpreneurship" which, in effect, is an extension of the "division profit centre" concept and is still unable to escape from the dominance of the general-management model.

Although "entrepreneurship" is already implanted in the "B" school curriculum, it will only be a different version of the same "general business management" or "business strategy" with no "entrepreneurial" substance in effect. An entrepreneurship course or program can only be of value in the educational process, if the following are observed:

1. It is clearly understood that entrepreneurship is a wealth-creation process and not merely applicable to profit-making business undertakings. The concept of entrepreneurship is applicable to all economic undertakings.
2. "Equity" is the basis for entrepreneurship development. The accumulation of equity is made up of contributions from all stakeholders, including cash investment and those investing passion, love and time for the creation, development and growth of the company.

3. Everyone in the organization/firm is both a stakeholder and a manager of his/her own task.

4. Individuals in the firm are responsible for creating wealth, adding value and generating desirable residuals for all stakeholders. An organization is assumed to be made up of people and money.

5. To transform the general-management model to an entrepreneurial model by developing:

    a. an extended equity concept to include people's contributions along with the financial contributions made by investors,

    b. human-resources economics to develop models to account for human value in all human endeavours.

The model can be illustrated further as follows:

Figure 2
Entrepreneurial model of management and its inter-relationship with stakeholders accounting and human-resources economics

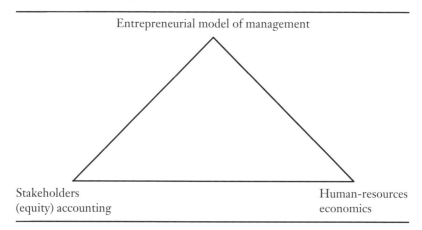

Entrepreneurial model of management

Stakeholders
(equity) accounting

Human-resources
economics

Conclusions

Entrepreneurship is appreciated by business and society as a wealth-creating and value-adding process, and its importance in business education has been recognized by business schools worldwide. Nonetheless, entrepreneurship education can be meaningful only if it can be created as an independent, academic discipline breaking away from the dominance of the general-management model, which assumes management to be separated from ownership. In an entrepreneurial management model, all individuals in the organization are stakeholders who recognize the human value in business which makes wealth creating and value adding the commitment of all individuals of the organization. The shift of paradigm should not merely be the adding of an entrepreneurship subject or program, but a fundamental change in the curriculum development philosophy; particularly, how to transform from general management to entrepreneurship by making a meaningful challenge to all "B" schools in our higher educational systems.

Source: Editorial, *Journal of Small Business & Entrepreneurship*, Vol. 11, No. 2, 1994, pp. 4–10.

6

All It is, is a Matter of Motivation

Thomas J. Peters and Robert H. Waterman Jr devoted thirty-one precious pages of their best-seller book In Search of Excellence *on the topic of "Man Waiting for Motivation". Since 1982, after more than a decade, man is still waiting for motivation. It appears that if the firm is still entrepreneurless, and management is separated from ownership, man will be waiting for motivation, possibly forever.*

Motivation: The Magic Word Used by People to Shape and Influence Others' Behaviour

We are responsive creatures by nature. Collectively and individually, we are motivated to be responsive, through internally generated needs, such as fear, comfort, expression of thoughts, feelings, and stored information. Externally, anything, even silence and darkness, will generate our response, including our climate and the surrounding environment. Hence, there is no such thing as an unmotivated individual. Behavioural scientists have provided valuable insight into the factors of motivation, and people's needs, but the bottom line is that it is impossible to motivate people to behave according to expectations unless their needs are satisfied. Politicians will not be elected if their political platforms are not approved by the voters (to meet their perceived needs); consumers will not consume, if advertisers fail to appeal to their needs. In the money-chasing game, advertisers have to be certain of what they advertise; a wrong message will not only hinder the selling of the products/services, but there is a possibility of back-firing, doing more damage than good. When Coca-Cola was playing around with changing the taste of Coca-Cola, and then reviving the old taste as Coca-Cola Classic, it must have cost the company a mint, and all because it had to find a way to satisfy consumers' need (Coke or Coca-Cola, that was the question). Similarly, Journey's End Hotel had to change its name to "Journey Hotel" because of the wrong message that "Journey's End" was sending to people. To some, "Journey's End" could mean the end of the journey, that is, life. Motivation is a powerful tool, and the key to motivation is knowing what people need.

Peters and Waterman, Jr (1982), like many others, know well what work means to people, and how it fulfils their needs. They said: "We desperately need meaning in our lives and will sacrifice a great deal to institutions that provide meaning to us. We simultaneously need independence, to feel as though we are in charge of our destinies, and to have the ability to stick it out." Can institutions provide meaning to the lives of those in the institutions? It is difficult to imagine how people can find meaning in life through working to achieve corporate goals, since it is only to satisfy shareholders' desired rate of return on their investment. If the big executives in the corporate entities do not recognize that working for the corporate goal does not necessarily satisfy people's needs, then under the circumstances, the working man (as noted in Peters and Waterman, Jr, 1982) may have to wait for motivation for a long time.

Everyone Seems to Know What Motivation is; The Challenge is "How"?

Behavioural scientists, management consultants and managers of corporations and other institutions, think, talk and want to motivate people at work. Titles, high or progressive remuneration, incentive plans, bonus systems, pension schemes, parking spaces, credit cards, large and well decorated offices, personal secretaries, computer facilities and among others, the key to the executive washroom, are supposedly incentives to motivate the individual to commit himself to good performance. In fact, the tri-polar behavioural theories X, Y and Z, are all dedicated to the purpose of finding who the individual is and how he or she behaves, so an appropriate human resources strategy can be derived to motivate people to work in accordance with the corporate or institutional executive's perception of what they are supposed to be working for.

Over the past four thousand years, the Chinese have had much to say about the meaning of life and among other things, wisdom about work, its needs and factors of motivation. In work, there are those who live to work, and those who work to live. People who live to work are workaholics who are not difficult to motivate because work itself is motivation. On the other hand, it is difficult to motivate those who work to live, for if they find a way to live without working, they will not work. The following is an example to illustrate the point.

Some years ago, I was invited to visit a Caribbean country to conduct a series of lectures on entrepreneurship. We (my wife and myself) were placed in a resort hotel. Through the entire period of approximately two weeks, I noticed a young man, without fail, fishing. It was strange to notice that he caught no more than three or four small fish at the end of the day. One day, I finished my lecture early and I had the opportunity to talk with him. Here is our conversation as I remember it:

Myself: Where are you working?

Fisherman: Working? What for?

Myself: If you are not working, are you going to school?

Fisherman: Going to school? What for?

Myself: Well, if you go to school, you may be able to secure a good job.

Fisherman: What for?

Myself: If you have a good job, or have a business of your own, you can make more money.

Fisherman: What for?

Myself: You can raise a family and save some money for the future.

Fisherman: What for?

Myself: If you have some money, you can retire from working and have a good life and do some fishing.

Fisherman: This is exactly what I am doing now.

You may not believe this story, but it is real, so real that I cannot help to think how naive I was. People are motivated by everything and anything, but not necessarily motivated by the same things, such as money and financial security, a job, a career and having your own business.

In China, factors of motivation are the subject of many old sayings which are so basic, yet virtually indisputable. One such old saying is: "People witness thousands of ships on the Yangtze River, travelling up and down stream everyday. The truth of the matter is, there are no thousand ships, but only two: one travels for name and the other for money." To the Chinese, this folk saying is a wisdom applicable to present day life, possibly everywhere in the world (perhaps the fisherman is an exception). It is no wonder that the key to the executive washroom (name), American Express card, the company's expense account, or year end bonus (money) seem to work well as motivation. But what about the millions and millions of people who are not privileged to have the key to the executive washroom, or a year end bonus? In any case, an executive washroom cannot be public domain otherwise how do we justify the word "executive"?

How are People Motivated?

As mentioned earlier, people can be motivated by anything and every-thing on earth and beyond: fortunately or unfortunately, fear of death is a factor of motivation. In fact, negative factors (including the fear of death) motivate people to be more effective than the positive ones. Although not publicized, the criminal codes of our civilized world are built entirely on the basis of negative reinforcement to our moral standards. People are motivated to respect the law through fear of losing their freedom (jail sentence or death penalty) or other forms of punishment (fine, suspension or cancellation of certain privileges). It may come as a surprise that it does not matter how civilized a country may be, there is no judicial system in the world that will provide incentives for people to do good. Religion does, on the other hand, but death must come first before canonization. If good deeds are not good enough to earn canonization, the reward for doing good is not on earth, but in heaven: Do not lay up for yourselves treasures upon earth. Where moth and rust destroy, and where thieves break in and steal. But lay up for yourselves treasures in heaven, where neither moth nor rust destroys, and where thieves do not break in or steal (Matthew 6:19–20).

If the law punishes the bad and in order to avoid punishment, people will not risk wrongdoing, then this is a factor of motivation: to motivate people to behave in accordance with the law and be good citizens.

In addition to our judicial system, religion also tends to motivate people through fear of unforeseen consequences beyond death. Through-out history, religions have been one of the greatest motivators for people to do good.

Motivation Works on Groups, as Well as Nations, so Long as We Know Their Collective Needs

"I Order You to Die"

During the Second World War, there was a Portuguese regiment surrounded by Germans. The Germans were fully aware that the Portuguese would soon surrender, not only because of military pressure but because the supplies in the regiment would not last, unless new supplies could reach them. Of course, it was clear that no supplies could pass through the German lines.

The morale of the Portuguese was low, and there was a clear sign that within a matter of days or even hours, the regiment would have to raise the white flag. Under international law, it was assumed that the prisoners of war would be properly treated. At a point when the decision had to be made: surrender or wait for rescue and fresh supplies, the commanding officer issued an order. It was a simple one: "I order you to die." The Portuguese soldiers fought hard, consequently they all died under gunfire. The story is not totally true because somebody had to survive the gunfire to tell the story.

Fear for Survival of the Race Motivated Japan

Japan's post-war economic success has been viewed all over the world as a remarkable achievement in history. In less than five decades, Japan rose from the unconditional surrender of its military to the Allies and military rule under the Americans, to become one of the economic powers of the world. This has made people tip their hats to their accomplishment. Many of us want to learn from them; even those who prefer not to take the trouble of learning from Japan are more or less curious to know what really makes the Japanese tick.

In the marketplace, it is not difficult to find books and other forms of materials devoted to exploring Japanese business strategies. There is conclusive evidence, as has been said by many people at different times, that the Japanese were able to capitalize on their post-war crisis by intensively restructuring their economy and forcing improvements in product designs, marketing techniques and manufacturing. In particular, they made every attempt to cut costs in order to stay profitable and competitive. There is also ample evidence that the Japanese have shown a talent for turning problems into opportunities. For example, when the oil crisis threatened the whole world, Japan was in a worse situation than anyone could imagine. For a country relying heavily on exports and industrial strength for global competition, without a fuel energy reserve and other possible natural resources to exploit, the Japanese were forced to rethink its economic strategy. They shifted their focus to electronics and computer technology. Moreover, the oil crisis also forced Japanese auto makers to produce more fuel-efficient cars. Both strategies worked for the Japanese. Japan is a leader in electronics technology and is one of the three prime auto making nations in the world. The Japanese success story is a puzzle to experts and laymen alike.

To explore Japan's success is no easy task. One must consider its history, the attributes of today's Japan as a whole, and among other things, its surrounding environment. Rather than follow the standard wisdom in exploring the style of Japanese business management, let us examine the more general aspect of the Japanese model such as the commitment of its people, and its long term employment philosophy. While the economic climate has made it necessary for Japanese firms to downsize and lay off people just as in Canada or the US, nevertheless, unemployment and employee turnaround is relatively low. One thing that is not often publicized is that the Japanese are great and fast learners. In Japan, there is a Japanization Theory that consists of two important schools of thought: the Confucian Management School adopted from China, and the Western Management School mostly influenced by the Americans. While they are imitators, the Japanese are also great adapters; when the Japanese learn something from other people, the outcomes are always better than the original. For example, through the 1980s and 1990s, much emphasis has been placed on Japan's efforts to strive for productivity and quality control for its products, but its strengths are mostly learned from American industries. As said by Yoshio Okawara (1982:3), the then Japanese Ambassador to the United States:

> It is no secret that Japanese management has for years been looking at, listening to, and learning from U.S. business, which continues to be the world's most dynamic and innovative. In fact, when you probe some of the strengths of Japanese industry today, such as in quality control and productivity, you will find that much of the original inspiration was derived from U.S. industry.

The doctrine of Confucianism in China at best is a political and social Humpty-Dumpty; some are all for it and others are vehemently against it. The establishment treats the doctrine like a Bible, revolutionists consider it a hindrance to progress, but it has had a strong influence on the Japanese in general, and business managers in particular. The following are some highlights of the Confucianism school of thought as interpreted by the Japanese (based on Murayama, 1982:109):

○ The group comes first and individuals must be willing to sacrifice or deny themselves for group doctrines.

○ The doctrines of Confucianism are interpretations of the spirit of God and to know one is to know the other.

○ From the viewpoint of decision making, harmony (*chowa*) is the first consideration and the virtue of the constant mean must be sought.

The Confucian doctrines have had an obvious effect on the Japanese commitment to the group good and have become part of the Japanese business value system. A similar commitment may not be as easy for some business persons in western countries to achieve. For example, after the Canadian government signed the Canadian and US Free Trade Agreement, and egged on by the beginning of a recession, a significant number of Canadian firms moved their operations down south of the border, including a company whose CEO was the chairperson of Canada's National Entrepreneurship Development Institute. Although there had been no clear evidence to suggest that operational costs would be cheaper than in Canada, the business migration cost Canada not only jobs but tax revenue as well. The commitment of these firms and their decision makers were certainly not to the group interest of Canada. This begs the following question: if the Japanese management system presumes a business value system so alien to the non-Japanese, what can we learn from it?

Geographically, Japan is a small country compared with its neighbours, China and Russia, or with many other countries across the Pacific and around the world. It has no significant natural resources, in particular, it lacks petroleum reserves, but its people share a common culture and tradition which emphasizes the common good of Japan. They are not afraid to learn from the "great" and strive to be the greatest of the great, but its people, individually and collectively, also share a common fear, the fear for the Japanese race. It is this fear for the survival of the Japanese race that motivates their desire to expand beyond Japan's natural boundary. One common folk saying in the eastern states: Japan has a little house, so the Japanese always want to visit other people's houses. This fear of racial survival is manifested in the deliberate distortion of modern history, particularly, in Japanese school textbooks. They are less than factual about the massacre of civilians in China and Southeast Asia during the war period from early 1930s thereon.

Westerners look at Japan's success and they see their huge profits as a result of what they perceive as unfair competitive practices and the ability to imitate the great ideas of others. What are seldom noted are Japanese business values and the impetus behind them.

Table 6.1 is a short list of sequential events that, in the author's opinion, have provided the greatest impetus for the current Japanese business strategy, always with the fear of survival which remains present in the back of the minds of the Japanese people.

Table 6.1
Events that provided the greatest impetus for the current Japanese business strategy

1945	World War II defeat and the unconditional surrender to the Allies that threatened Japan's survival.
1945	Immediate Allied (mostly American) military occupation that humiliated Japan's national pride and put into question their belief in their racial superiority. On the other hand, it provided a great opportunity for its government to reassess its world competitive strategy. With the aid of the US, both government and private sector business investment interests emerged.
1974	Oil crisis threatened Japan's industrial expansion strategy. This turned out to be an opportunity as it resulted in a restructuring of its industrial strategy from manufacturing to electronics. Although the computer microchip business originated in Silicon Valley in the US, the Japanese will eventually capture the world market. The oil crisis also provided Japanese auto makers with the opportunity to build and market more fuel-efficient cars to gain leadership in the auto industry.
1993–1994	The acceleration of capital accumulation both at home and abroad coupled with a deferred recession (from the west) have made Japanese business leaders and the government rethink and reshape its economic strategy.

What the Japanese have done best, more often than not, is to get into the deepest water, and then somehow stand on that water to see over everyone else's heads; they turn problems into opportunities.

For years, westerners have thought that the Japanese economic success would not last. Many have felt and suggested that Japan would end up with the same US-style consumer driven society and suffer the same recessional consequences as did the US and other western countries. This did not happen in Japan and it is unlikely to happen because its motivational factors are quite different from that of westerners, particularly amongst its business people. Westerners are motivated by profit and achieving a desirable rate of return on shareholders' investment. The Japanese are also for profit, but motivation depends on more than just profit. The commitment to the common good and the fear for racial survival are all part of the motivational forces that have made Japan what it is.

The Determination to Overcome Humiliation as a Factor of Motivation

Taiwan is an island which is two-thirds rocks and mountains and very little in the way of natural resources. Despite its handicaps, Taiwan has become a remarkable economic success during the past three decades, following the retreat of the Nationalists to the island, after the success of the Maoists in China in the late 1940s. In the author's opinion, it is this event that has made Taiwan what it is, along with the endurance and determination to overcome humiliation learned by its government and people during the past five decades.

The sequence of events speak for themselves. These include the withdrawal from mainland China in 1948–49; losing its seat as a permanent member of the Security Council of the United Nations in October 1971 and withdrawal of its representation from the world body at the same time; the termination of official diplomatic relations with virtually every other country in the world (more or less saying: "I won't play with you any more"), except Costa Rica, South Africa and a few other smaller nations. Just imagine, if you were from Taipei and happened to be in New York visiting the UN; you would have witnessed the lowering of your national flag from the front of the UN building. How would you feel? You have been rejected by the United Nations, an organization which supposedly represents every single living human being on earth.

Humiliation has made Taiwan self-reliant and spurred on a search for economic strength to sustain its national pride. It may take a revolution to win political freedom, but only entrepreneurial spirit is needed to gain economic freedom. The Nationalists in Taiwan may never return to mainland China, but through its entrepreneurial mindset and its determination to overcome humiliation, Taiwan has become an economic miracle.

The Tiananmen Square Incident Threw China's Political Progress Backwards but Advanced China's Economic Growth

China, the mother dragon of all dragons, was motivated to pursue its economic growth quite differently. First, the nation as a whole was motivated by its struggle out of poverty, an inherent factor which is the result of a series of historical misfortunes. When the whole country was just about to raise its head and say to the world: "We can do it", the Tiananmen Square incident caught everyone by surprise. To the West, and perhaps the whole world, it was an unfortunate tragedy which not only pushed China's political progress back twenty years (to the time of the Cultural Revolution), but also its economic progress, particularly its trade relations with other nations. Although it was not part of China's economic planning, the incident created an opportunity of awareness and opportunity for its people to realize this reality of life. It would not be possible to change its political environment immediately after the Tiananmen Square incident but it might be possible for them to gain economic freedom and freedom from poverty through entrepreneurship, since entrepreneurship works under any system, as long as the government does not take the entire harvest.

The key events in China's economic progress before and after the Tiananmen Square incident as the author sees it are: On 1 October 1949, China's Communist leaders led by Chairman Mao Zedong proclaimed the birth of the People's Republic of China. Within a period of less than twenty years, a leadership struggle led to political unrest and a new wave of revolution, the Cultural Revolution, which as we know, was intended to wipe out the four "olds": old ideas, old culture, old customs and old habits. When it ended in 1976, China was left with virtually no economic means to make it a business partner in the world economy. When a new leadership assumed power after the Cultural Revolution, they had a vision of a modern, industrialized China. In 1978, Deng Xiaoping announced the first outline of plans to set China on the road to recovery.

For a country with a population of over 1.3 billion and uneven availability of resources, central planning is not only preferable but unavoidable. On the other hand, in order to create wealth and add value, economic reform would have to be carried out on the industrial and urban level, particularly, in moving away from mandatory planning and making more use of guidance planning and the influence of market forces. This has increasingly been done since 1984. China moved onto urban and industrial reform cautiously with the main thrusts as follows:

1. To delegate administration and supervision of economic enterprise to the lower levels within the boundaries of local economic policies and planning.
2. To make each enterprise responsible for its profit and loss.
3. To give managers of each enterprise market responsibilities so they can act in accordance with conditions in the marketplace.
4. To give managers of each enterprise the responsibility to acquire needed resources and to secure their own sales outlets.
5. To provide enterprises with incentives for good performance, both for the individual and the enterprise.
6. To allow profits to be retained in the enterprise, managers or directors were given the authority to control financial resources.

7. To judge performances by productivity, efficiency and effective use of the resources to achieve enterprise goals, rather than the ideological criteria prior to 1976, the end of the Cultural Revolution.

8. To give enterprises considerable freedom to develop their own market and set their own prices controlled principally by market forces, namely supply and demand.

Source: A summary of materials supplied by the State Council Overseas Affairs Office, China.

In 1989, the author was invited by China's State Commission of Education to conduct a lecture tour from north to south. During the tour, the author had the opportunity to interact with a large number of people with different backgrounds including academics, business leaders of China's state enterprises as well as representatives from foreign companies doing business in China, local entrepreneurs, non-communist political party leaders, people holding key positions in public offices, association leaders, people in the street, villagers and students. We discussed life in China, particularly matters about business and China's economic future. The following is a summary of the discussion:

1. China, a large country with approximately 1.3 billion people, has a general consensus to gain its economic freedom by developing, cultivating and nurturing the entrepreneurial spirit.

2. The world cannot afford to have a weak China; with China in a stronger position, it could contribute greatly to the world economy.

3. China's need is not merely to earn export dollars to strengthen its balance of payment, but also to develop a domestic consumer's market. This will have twofold benefits, with industrial development and entrepreneurship giving China the opportunity to work toward its economic freedom and providing surplus time and money to improve the standard of living, and in turn helping the world economy.

4. China does not need foreign aid but asks for the right to do business. The Chinese want to earn their economic freedom, not ask for charity.

5. China's task is to utilize its massive human resources to create wealth and add value. The period of shouting political slogans and banner waving are over. A commitment has been made to make China a rich and prosperous nation and with a market system that works in the West and Pacific countries.

6. Taiwan has a one-party dominant system which works. Although the Nationalist Party in the dominant position runs the government

there are other parties, small and unnoticed by outsiders, which function as watch dogs. The one-party dominant system also appears to be workable in China. This does not mean that the system will not change, but if change is made, it will be done, not because outsiders want it, but because the Chinese want it themselves.

A similar view of the future of China's economic reforms was expressed by executives of subsidiaries of foreign multinationals. Proctor and Gamble's general manager stationed in South China said: "We know it is difficult for us to have a profitable operation at the moment but doing business in China is a long shot, an investment opportunity we couldn't afford to miss. But we feel quite comfortable about the whole situation. In a sense, we are now at the end of the tunnel." To do business with China is an "in thing". Just by looking at the services provided by reputable professional firms such as Price Waterhouse, Deloitte Haskins & Sells, and financial institutions such as the Hongkong Bank and the Standard Chartered Bank, it is not difficult to appreciate the reality that China is on the verge of economic recovery.

When China's economic reforms were just about to take off, the Tiananmen Square incident occurred. The incident was viewed by outsiders as a serious blow to China's political and economic progress, especially in its trade relations with the US. The people in China were even more devastated. It was a regrettable incident from any viewpoint, but the incident did motivate China to be more determined to push through its economic reforms. It was not possible for China to change external opinions of its political reality, but China's economic reality could change as it continued to pursue opportunities to stimulate entrepreneurial drive and liberalize barriers to induce foreign investment. The following measures reflect how China is turning problems into opportunities for its rapid economic reforms:

1. Designation of economic development areas to serve as models for the transformation from a command economy to a market economy.
2. The creation of a number of stock exchanges in selected cities, with the expectation of developing Shanghai as the financial centre for China.
3. The appointment of a non-communist industrialist as a state vice-president.
4. The easing of price control.
5. Co-operation with Singapore to develop model regions.
6. The liberalization of foreign exchange and consolidation of the dual currency system.

Three years after the Tiananmen Square incident, China made a remarkable comeback on its economic performance. In the author's opinion, if the Tiananmen Square incident pushed China's political status back twenty years, it motivated China's desire to push for economic reform, thereby propelling its economic growth thirty years ahead. In a way, there is clear evidence supporting China's intention to tell the world: "We know we are right, economic freedom must come first. If the political system needs to be changed, changes will be made because China needs it, not because outsiders say so."

Motivation: The Individual and the Individual's Needs

Some 2,000 years ago, Confucius grasped the essence of people's needs, when he said: "Food and sex are human nature." This seems to make a lot of sense but neither he nor any of his followers through the centuries attempted to make it into a theory. Hence, Confucius is not quite known as a behavioural scientist or a candidate for a Nobel prize in the humanities. Never copyrighted, this theory of basic needs has become part of the domain of pop culture and restaurant commercials. On the other hand, westerners, particularly Americans and most particularly American psychologists, have made an industry out of defining the various needs of an individual. Maslow, for example, was pivotal in making the study of human needs into a management discipline. According to Maslow (1954: Chap. 5), needs can be classified into five categories:

- Physiological
- Safety, stability, and security
- Belongingness and love
- Self-esteem and the esteem of others
- Self-actualization, self-realization, and self-accomplishment

Maslow, along with a few others (such as D. C. McClelland and Clayton P. Alderfer), was responsible for providing the basis of the hierarchy of needs theory of human motivation. In this theory, the basic needs of the individual must be fulfilled first or else an individual will not strive for high needs. The theory has been widely used to guide business managers and other decision makers to form their human resources management policies.

From the basis of the hierarchy of needs theory, researchers and practitioners have classified a variety of needs. These needs are acquired as a result of specific circumstances. These include the need for pride, the need for justice and the need for financial advancement to raise a family, for children's education, or for a death in the family. Speculations about future events could also motivate an individual to express unusual behaviour. Other needs developed by Alderfer (1972) to revise Maslow's needs theory along with his research findings include existence needs (much the same as Maslow's physiological and safety needs), relatedness needs (similar to Maslow's love or belongingness needs), esteem needs of an interpersonal nature, and growth needs (Maslow's esteem needs and self-actualization).

How does the needs theory work? It works on everything and anything that one wishes it to work for. The challenge is to identify people's needs. People can be motivated once the need(s) is (are) satisfied. There is one incident that can illustrate this point.

Some years ago, at an international conference, a well-known personality spoke about motivation and how people can be motivated to do what management expected them to do. By the end of his talk, he had impressed the audience with his expertise in human resources management, and hence a large number of participants were motivated to raise their hands and ask questions. One participant came to the microphone and asked the speaker: "I have a hundred-million-dollar business, and I seem to have no way to motivate my managers to be more entrepreneurial and take initiative in the interest of the company. Would you consider being my consultant?"

The speaker asked him: "What is there for me in return for being your consultant?"

The participant said: "Name your price, $100,000 or even $500,000."

The speaker reacted: "I don't want your money, but I am going to give you a tip without charging you a cent. I will be your consultant if you could restore me a full head of hair."

The speaker was bald, with a head shining like a lighted light bulb under the flood-lights projecting onto the podium.

The above is a simple illustration showing that you cannot motivate people to work if you do not know people's needs. The speaker's need was not the basics as advocated by Confucius, but the high need for self-esteem. Yet who would know under the circumstances? The fact is he was not joking. The speaker revealed to the author all the ordeals he endured while trying to restore his hair, including: transplants, special solutions, thermal treatment, massages, medicated shampoos, expert consultations all over the world; everything and anything except the use of a toupee. He could not imagine having a toupee on top of his head, not only because his shiny bald head provided no traction for the toupee to have a strong hold but because he could not stand the image.

In another example of needs theory, let us look at the Canadian unemployment insurance national scheme at work.

The unemployment insurance scheme is a national programme designed to provide relief for those unfortunate victims of plant shut-downs, downsizing, and structure change or simply laying off because of seasonal business fluctuations. The scheme works well in providing for basic needs, but unfortunately, it works so well that it discourages people from seeking employment. Some unemployed workers prefer to collect the benefit even when work is available; they would ask their potential employers to sign the paper of refusal to provide employment so they can continue to rely on the unemployment insurance benefits. This is not a criticism; it is an illustration. Those people who work to live would live without working as the system of relying on unemployment insurance benefits provides no motivation for them to work to satisfy other needs, unless it is to satisfy their need for achievement and self-esteem, etc. Perhaps this is the reason why a need for achievement is an entrepreneurial attribute.

What Motivates People Wanting to Start up Their Own Business?

During the period when the author was involved in teaching entre-preneurship and the small business development programme at the Ryerson Polytechnic University, Canada (then Ryerson Polytechnic Institute), the author conducted a survey of students' intentions with respect to their career choice over a period of six years. The results for those intending to start up a business are given in Table 6.2.

Table 6.2
A survey of career choice among final year students. Class (sample) size: between 28 to 35 students

	Financial gains		Independence		Others	
	Male %	Female %	Male %	Female %	Male %	Females %
1981	81	17	16	81	3	2
1982	80	14	18	80	2	6
1983	82	10	10	85	8	5
1984	81	11	15	82	4	7
1985	84	14	12	80	4	6
1986	83	16	12	81	5	3

The survey result is by no means conclusive. It does reflect how individuals perceive their personal reasons for starting up a business. While male students tend to be motivated by financial gains, female students on the other hand, perceive independence to be more important than financial gains. If this survey were to be conducted on other groups with a totally different background or at a different time (such as recession time, or at a time when environmental variables favour entrepreneurship or self-employment), or even at different places, the result could be different.

There is no consensus that one can verify why people want to have businesses of their own. There are research findings and literature that can just as well justify their claims for reasons of financial gains, independence, and/or simply because of love and passion for one's own work and creation. There is also clear evidence that by and large people are motivated by positive reasons (gains) just as much as by negative ones (to escape an uncomfortable environment). In the introduction of their book, Chan Kwok Bun and Claire Chiang state:

> It also came out throughout our four years of writing this book. That individuals are subject to the influence and control of external, impersonal forces is only half of the story. The other half necessarily draws our attention to the human ability to form new meanings and new lines of action, to modify these influences, and to change, often not alone, but *with* others, socially ... (1994: 18).

Among a large number of works involved in the search for why individuals start up their own businesses, Russell M. Knight (1983) provides an interesting insight on entrepreneurship in Canada. In essence, the findings suggest that those entrepreneurs under his study were not primarily motivated by financial incentives, but wanted to escape an uncomfortable environment and find new meaning in life for themselves. In summary, he concluded his findings by reporting the following classifications:

1. **The foreign refugee**. The most obvious escapee is the refugee from another country who has come to North America to escape political or religious persecution or to seek an economy with greater opportunities.

2. **The corporate refugee**. This individual has become dissatisfied with the corporate environment in which he worked previously. He feels he would increase his job satisfaction tremendously by starting and operating his own business.

3. **The parental (paternal) refugee**. Individuals obtained business training and experience through the family environment and

working in the family business. A significant number of such children, however, find their entrepreneurial fathers quite domineering and are attempting to escape from them in starting their own businesses, often in different fields from the family firm.

4. **The feminist refugee.** The feminist who feels she is discriminated against by male superiors, peers, and subordinates in the educational system, the corporate environment and society in general, starts her own business to escape from discrimination.

5. **The housewife refugee.** The housewife or home-maker, who often looks after her family until the children have grown at least to school age, decides to go back to work and start her own business, usually with her family's assistance.

6. **The society refugee.** The classic cases of this phenomenon are artists, sculptors, craftsmen and others who do not agree with many of the aspects of their society. They often start businesses which are tied to their craft, hobby or artistic skills.

7. **The educational refugee.** Many people who drop out or fall out of our educational system start their own business.

The list is by no means complete and individuals in developing countries whose reasons for starting their own business could be quite different from those in developed countries. To gain economic freedom is perhaps the reason for many of our entrepreneurs. At least in one country, there is concern for the displacement of aged prostitutes and starting a business of their own seems to be a sensible alternative under the circumstances.

When the question of "reasons for starting up one's own business" was given to a group of MBA students at the Nanyang Technological University, their unanimous opinion was that their forefathers went into business for survival, in a sense to obtain basic economic freedom in a foreign land. In today's affluent society where professionals are being well rewarded for their services, there is nothing to prompt individuals with high education to consider shifting into another career stream. In the words of Richard Cantillon, it is going into "self-employment with an uncertain return".

Motivation of People at Work

The socialist ideal failed: people will not work for the good of the state or to achieve a classless society. In the capitalist world, most people work for themselves and for a better life. There are exceptions: some make "working for others" a lifetime career. On the other hand, this can be as rewarding as being the huntsmen's dog: after bringing back the catch, the dog has to watch as the huntsmen feast, and then it is thrown a bone as its reward. The truth of the matter is that working under the capitalist system may not be that bad. On the other hand, there are unmotivated people, just as Peters and Waterman, Jr say: "men waiting for motivation … We desperately need meaning in our lives and will sacrifice a great deal to institutions that provide meaning for us." The question is: can institutions provide meaning for those working under the corporate banner? Will we work in order to attain the goal of the firm, namely, to maximize the rate of return on shareholders' investment?

7

The Missing Ingredients: Ownership and Decision Making

"Who owns the earth?" A teacher asked her grade one pupils. One child responded: "We do!" Another child disagreed: "No, we don't, God does."

Ownership: Who Owns the Earth?

In a grade one class in a remote northern village in Canada, the teacher talked about the environment, the place we live in, the beautiful land, sky, the lovely birds, the playful animals … Suddenly, the teacher raised a question to her pupils: "Children, tell me, who owns the earth?"

Susan raised her hand without hesitation and said to her teacher: "We own it!"

Then the teacher asked her: "Why? How do you know we own the earth?"

Susan responded by saying: "Every year near Christmas time, Coca-Cola has all the children in the world singing 'We are the world'. Since we are the world ourselves, and the world is the earth, I figured we must own it."

Her response immediately attracted an objection from another pupil, Bob. He said: "No, we don't! Nobody owns the world, but God does." The teacher asked him why and Bob said: "When my father died last year, my mum and the minister in the church told me: 'God called him back to heaven.' So I figured everything on earth and the earth itself belong to God."

His answer made another pupil, Jeffrey, raise his hand. He said: "Teacher, Susan is right, we own the earth, because earth is our home; Neil Armstrong told us so when he was in space."

Jeffrey elaborated: "When Neil Armstrong was in the spaceship in space and looked at the earth, he said: 'Ah! Earth, our home.' How can it not be ours, if it is our home?"

Mary did not agree with Jeffrey. She said: "Teacher, I don't know if I should agree with Jeffrey. Last year we came to Canada from ——, and my dad said to me: 'We cannot go back to see grandpa and grandma, because —— is not our home anymore.' How come? If earth is our home, why shouldn't —— be our home too?"

Mary's parents emigrated to Canada with refugee status. In a sense, they came away from their homeland to escape from political prosecution. Mary could not figure out how the earth could be "our home", yet the place that had been her home since she was born, was no longer home any more? Mary was puzzled.

Who Owns the Earth: Do We or Don't We?

The pupils' interaction in class made the teacher begin to wonder herself: Who owns planet earth? Rather than answering the question directly, it might be interesting to examine our reality in ways we do not normally perceive.

There is no doubt that the corporate structure is a dream child of a happy marriage between accounting and economics, and is the key player in the capitalistic society. So, let us borrow the corporate idea and assume the entire planet earth is a huge corporation. There is some merit to this, since like corporate entities, the earth has an infinite life span compared with the human beings on it and is less affected by the decisions and actions of the individual. The question is: while shareholders hold the ownership of the corporation, who is the rightful owner of the "Corporation of Planet Earth" (CPE)?

The owners of Corporation of Planet Earth are its shareholders and the shareholders are all living things on earth. The corporation provides its shareholders with everything they need to survive on this planet. Indeed, like all corporate shareholders, they require not just survival, but also a desirable rate of return on investment. The ROI to CPE shareholders is no other than the planet's ability to continue to replenish itself (a similar idea to capital replenishment) and provide a better life for the future of all inhabitants on earth (a similar idea to the profit required by business corporations). CPE's managers are the human race who are requested to observe the goals of the corporation and are given specific responsibilities, rights and entitlements as stated in Table 7.1. CPE is different from most other corporations in that without the managers, it would continue to run perfectly well on its own. Our role as managers is self-appointed, so we have no one to blame but ourselves if we prove incompetent.

CPE's corporate goals are:

- The rivers must always run clean.
- The air must always be fresh.
- People can step lightly upon the Earth.
- People can always live with reverence.
- The earth continues to be a sacred place.

On the basis of the preceding discussion, at the beginning of life, we may construct a balance sheet as in Figure 7.1.

Table 7.1
The responsibilities and rights of CPE's managers

Responsibilities	Rights
To ensure that capital remains intact	The entitlement to good remuneration
To earn a desirable return to CPE's shareholders as stated in the corporation's goal, and to ensure profit is used for the continuation of life and the improvement of life support systems for its inhabitants now and in the future	The right to make decisions to allocate resources in the interest of all living creatures on the planet now and in the future
	To create a world for humans and all other living creatures to live together in harmony and prosperity. In this case, prosperity means freedom from poverty, freedom from sickness and freedom from fear and injustice

Figure 7.1

Corporation of Planet Earth
Balance Sheet
As of day 1, years ago

ASSETS		LIABILITY	
Sunshine	xxxx trillion	Future generations	0
Water	xxxx trillion		
Fresh air	xxxx trillion		
Plants (the green environment)	xxxx trillion		
Underground mineral deposits	xxxx trillion	Shareholders' equity	7 x xxxx trillion
Soil and all its nutrients	xxxx trillion		
All other living beings	xxxx trillion	Total liability and shareholders' equity	7 x xxxx trillion
All other assets	xxxx trillion		
Total assets	7 x xxxx trillion		

Note: x denotes unspecified great numbers.

Before massive exploitation by humans of resources and life support for the living beings on earth, the corporation had no liabilities to future generations because there was enough of everything to support the future. Since humans assumed the stewardship of managing the planet, it has been found that the planet is in serious danger of losing its life support capabilities for humans and all other living beings.

If the balance sheet of CPE were to be drawn up today, it would have a large liability which means that much of the assets have diminished over the years. Whereas no real additional investment has been added to CPE, the so-called profit has been in reality a depletion of capital. Under the circumstances, what the extremely rich and well-to-do individuals lavishly spend on and waste are not profits, but part of the capital. The new balance sheet is shown in Figure 7.2.

The illustration shows that we have so poorly managed the planet to the extent that we have depleted our life support and incurred a huge liability borrowed from our future generations.

Unlike other corporations, our shareholders cannot call a shareholders' meeting nor make any formal protest about our poor performance, but they have gradually and more rapidly in recent years expressed disenchantment about what has been done to the corporation. The auditor's report is in; it tells us of some serious consequences:

Figure 7.2

Corporation of Planet Earth
Balance Sheet
31 December 1993

ASSETS		LIABILITY	
Sunshine	xx trillion	Future	
Water	xx trillion	generations	7 x x trillion
Fresh air	xx trillion		
Plants (the green environment)	xx trillion		
Underground deposits	xx trillion	Shareholders' equity	7 x xxxx trillion
Soil and all its nutrients	xx trillion	Less: Accumulated operating loss	(7 x xxx trillion)
All other living beings	xx trillion	Net shareholders' equity	7 x x trillion
All other assets	xx trillion	Total liability and shareholders' equity	
Total assets	7 x xx trillion		7 x xx trillion

Notes:

1. Both balance sheets (Figures 7.1 and 7.2) have been drawn up for illustration purposes, and they are not necessarily arithmetically or mathematically correct.

2. The liability of the corporation will increase at a very rapid rate, as the population increases exponentially.

3. There is no clear evidence that the shareholders of CPE will induce new investment. Therefore, the assets depletion is a reality unless creative and innovative efforts are extended to create new assets from existing assets. The only other alternative is to emigrate to other planets or venture into the unknown which is not immediately predictable.

- ○ Rapid decrease of corporation's assets
- ○ Rapid decrease in the ability of the corporation to replenish the lost assets
- ○ Water pollution
- ○ Acid rain
- ○ Ozone depletion
- ○ Global warming
- ○ Drain on underground deposits
- ○ Disappearance of many rightful inhabitants of the earth
- ○ Loss of our ancient tropical rain forests along with thousands of valuable species
- ○ Other unreported losses

In addition, the auditor prepared a graphic expression with respect to our support system as shown in Figure 7.3.

The question is: why have we so poorly managed our planet if we are the owners of our planet? Why do we not care for the future of the planet, the only means to sustain our life and the lives of our children and grandchildren? Perhaps an ancient story may help us.

Many years ago, two women appealed to King Solomon for the ownership of a beautiful child. One woman's tears ran down her face like water from the Mississippi river, and the other bowed her head down, made no sound, but repeated two simple words very quietly: "My baby, my baby." To King Solomon, both appeared to be genuine and either one could have been the rightful mother of the child. However, the judgement had to be made.

Figure 7.3
Graphic expression, life support system (Source: Foreword in Clifton and Turner, 1990)

If a lily pond contains a single leaf on the first day and every day the number of leaves doubles, when is the pond half full, if it is completely full in thirty days? The answer is the twenty-ninth day.

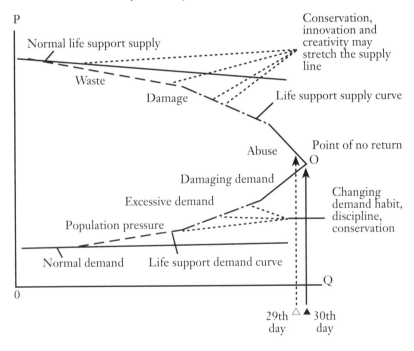

After a short pause, the king made his decision. He said to the women: "I sympathize with both of you, and you have both impressed me as being the real mother of the child, but we have only one child. In order to be fair to both of you, I am going to cut the child in two halves, and each one of you will have one half of the child." The woman who was in tears became even more emotional and said to the king: "Oh! Your great divinity, what justice, thank you, thank you. Since I cannot have the child all to myself, I am happy with your judgement to have one half of the child." The other woman, on the other hand, appeared to be shocked by the king's judgement. She bowed to the king, knocked her head on the ground and appealed to the king: "My great lord, please, please let the other woman have the child." I am sure, we all realize who the child's real mother was. It was her love and care of the child that made her the real mother (the owner) of this little human being.

If humans are the real owners of the planet, we must have love and passion for what we own. What is surprising is that in one respect, we seem to have claimed and assumed the ownership of the planet, yet on the other hand, we behave like irresponsible tenants of the planet. We steal corporate assets, cheat our shareholders, and worst of all, we disfranchise our children and grandchildren of their right to live. Therefore, who owns the earth is not at issue; the issue is whether we consider ourselves merely passersby who should grab whatever we can, or owners of our home, responsible possessors of what nature provided us. The answer is obvious: love, care and passion come along with ownership. Like the woman in King Solomon's judgement story, the real mother (owner of the child) cared and loved enough that she preferred to let the other woman have the child: to give up ownership in order to save the child. The other woman was certainly not the mother (owner) of the child. All she wanted was to grab whatever she could, to the extent of letting the child be cut in two halves, so she could have one half of the dead child whom she claimed to be her own.

The Ownership Package: Passion, Love and Care

Ownership affects every human being. There has been ample evidence to support the claim that we care and love what we own, and we are indifferent to properties (or possessions) owned by others. The most obvious experience that anyone can have is to compare a public washroom (toilet) and a washroom at home. For some strange reason, in the men's washroom, you can never find a dry space in front of a urinal, and litter and tissue paper are found all over the floor, even though there are wastepaper baskets nearby. There are other unspeakable circumstances that could turn one's stomach upside down. On the other hand, everyone including people with little means, keep their own washrooms at home clean, free from odour, and often decorated with flowers and ornaments. The difference, of course, lies in ownership. Casual users and passersby tend to be indifferent to their surroundings, while owners tend to take good care of what they possess. As a matter of interest, the following two little stories demonstrate how individuals care about their ownership to the extent of making themselves slaves to their possessions.

The Bicycle Story

This story tells of a person who purchased a new bicycle. He cared about the bicycle so much, he washed, cleaned and polished it on a daily basis. He was worried that the road might dirty it, and there might even be a slight chance the bicycle would accidentally be damaged. He loved the vehicle so much that he decided to preserve it as long as he could, so he decided not to ride on it to work, but carried it on his shoulder instead.

The Fan Story

This is another interesting story about an old man who loved his newly purchased fan made of bamboo and paper that could be folded or opened. Three years later, his friend saw him with the same fan in his hands but as fresh and new as before. His friend asked him: "Why is your fan so new when mine, which I acquired only a few months ago, is already out of shape and partly ripped?" The old man told his friend: "Oh, it's simple, I keep it so well, and I will show you how." He opened his fan, but instead of moving his fan left and right, he held his fan still and moved his head.

What the two stories tell us may appear to be extreme, or fantasized incidents, but there is wisdom in both stories. They tell us how far people can go with respect to ownership, protecting their possessions and ending up being the slaves to the possessions.

Over the years, in the author's personal experiences serving as a consultant to many entrepreneur-managed businesses, it was found that with rare exception, entrepreneurs tended to refuse venture capitalists' financing to support their firms' growth. It was all because they feared losing the effective control of the firm. They perceived that erosion of their ownership would be the result if venture capitalists were involved. Among the various financing options, from money suppliers (the bankers), investors (venture capitalists) and partners, bank financing is still the single largest source of financing because it does not affect their equity holdings. This is despite the fact that bank financing tends to put cash flow pressure onto the firm's financial position for the same reason. The entrepreneurs have very little tolerance for financing from anyone that will have a tendency to affect their ownership over the business.

Ownership Acquisition

There are many ways to acquire ownership. The individual can work for it, purchase it, exchange it, negotiate for it, grab it in the presence of opportunity, or as exhibited in the earlier part of our history, use gunboats and military invasion. In fact, the entire colonial and imperialistic mentality is built on the basis of acquiring ownership. The British, Japanese, French, Dutch, Spanish and Portuguese all had their share of acquiring ownership through colonization. As an added form of land acquisition, during the pioneer days, pioneers from the old countries landed in North America to acquire land ownership, sometimes through trading with the natives (who rarely had the same conception of owner-ship) using any attractive goods, including mirrors, cloth, jewellery or even smoking pipes, or often through a decree from the crown (many died from hardship or fought with the natives and/or other explorers). Land ownership could be acquired simply by having the fastest horse and staking claims on the land before others had a chance.

The use of gunboat diplomacy and military operations to colonize other people's lands and acquire ownership are out of fashion these days, partially due to our realization that we must not do harm to others for the sake of acquiring ownership, but also because our world body, the United Nations, serves as the watchdog to alert us not to repeat what we had wrongly done before. People of the twenty-first century will have to accept the idea that hard work, creativity and innovation are the way to add value to society and acquire ownership in the process.

Ownership, in a sense, is the reward for creativity and innovation. Ownership is awarded to an entrepreneur for the creation of a business, just as writers, artists, inventors and other creative individuals are awarded ownership through patent and copyright protection. The writers, artists and inventors all have the right to make decisions on the ownership and enjoy the harvest.

Other than what has already been described above, in practice, ownership means virtually everything and anything that one can imagine. We own our personal possessions, our own name, titles, honours, and in democratic countries, the right to vote and be voted into public offices. Some of these forms of ownership are not saleable or transferable, while others are marketable or transferable. In addition, there is also symbolic ownership or ownership of honours extended to individuals who had made great contributions or added great value to society, such as through having a street, building and/or university named after them. Although ownership of honours is given on the basis of the individual's creative and innovative contributions, normally they are not directly associated with entrepreneurship or entrepreneurial endeavours, since entrepreneurship is commonly linked to business or business-like activities.

While investors acquiring business ownership generally purchase shares of desirable corporations through the stock market, the creative individuals who desire to acquire ownership on the other hand, would normally go through the process of starting up a business. Most people consider starting up a business will require money, business ideas and market opportunity. The fact is that to acquire ownership by starting up one's own business, one needs a great deal more than money, business ideas and the presence of market opportunity. There is also such a thing as strategic fit, which includes:

- the product
- the market opportunity
- availability of financial resources
- personal preferences and capability
- availability of human resources
- willingness to make sacrifices on the part of the entrepreneur
- timing
- environmental consideration
- legal framework
- others

Almost without exception, there is a great deal of personal sacrifice involved in starting up a new venture, not only just the opportunity cost for the individual, but often a change in the entire lifestyle. However, it is still worth it; simply by acquiring ownership through your own business, you will make decisions for yourself and develop not only passion and love for your business, but everything in the business, including people, resources and the environment. In summation, it gives a different kind of economic freedom, one you cannot expect to have as an employee of a large corporation.

The Possessive Nature of Ownership

To acquire ownership is, in effect, the right to make decisions: the decisions to allocate resources, the decisions for the owner's self-interest, and more often than not, the decisions for others who are attached or related to the possession. To protect and preserve the right to make decisions, ownership must include possession. Possession can be observed from people's interactions, business dealings and conflicts. In more serious cases, excessively exercising the right to possess can be extremely harmful; it may even result in tragedies beyond comprehension. The following incident illustrates the point.

In the spring of 1980, in the author's old home in Markham, Ontario, the author's neighbour on the right was digging holes to stake fence poles. For reasons unknown, his neighbour in the back complained to him that the holes he was digging were about six inches into his side of the property. They argued, then got into a heated exchange. As the exchange continued, the noise drew other neighbours, including the author, to the site, and they witnessed the fight. A few minutes later, with no solution to the dispute, the neighbour at the back suddenly became short of breath, and died on the spot because of heart failure. Why a person is willing to risk his life and fight for a few inches of land is beyond comprehension since everything ends with death. The incident, nevertheless, demonstrates how individuals can be so possessed by the idea of ownership that they end up giving up their right to live.

The "Jekyll and Hyde" Ownership

In the West, there is a classic story by Robert Louis Stevenson entitled *Dr Jekyll and Mr Hyde*. It is about one man with two personalities, one good, and the other, evil. The Chinese have a thought and the basis for a philosophy similar to Dr Jekyll and Mr Hyde, known as "ying and yang". Dr Jekyll and Mr Hyde expressed an aspect of ying and yang philosophy because it refers to the reality of life that everything has two sides, the good and the evil.

On the Dr Jekyll (the good) side of ownership, you can use your ownership to your satisfaction; it involves passion, love, care and sharing or any other good deed. Mother Teresa, with her love for humanity, gave her Nobel prize award money to the poor and disadvantaged. In the business world, virtually without exception, entrepreneurs always take great care of their businesses. The entrepreneurs' personal feelings, passion and love are not only extended to their businesses, but to their employees as well. The late John Bulloch, father of John F. Bulloch, President of the Canadian Federation of Independent Business, left as his last words on earth to his children the request to take care of the firm's (John Bulloch Tailors) employees. The Inuit communities in North America, unknown to many outsiders, also had a beautiful tradition (the author has no knowledge whether it is still in practice today) of sharing ownership which was in the form of sharing the harvests, the fruit of their labour, with those who were unable to labour because of age or other misfortunes.

In the days of hunting and fishing for a living, Inuits had their own way of giving recognition to hunters even though the older hunters were no longer able to hunt. The recognition given to the elders was a simple gesture: Once a hunter brought back his catch, the elders were asked to place their hands on the animal, and thus ownership was recognized, and the elders got their share of the harvest.

The bad (Mr Hyde) side of ownership represents greed, cheating, killing, exploiting others and the environment as reflected in people's behaviour. When bulldozers razed the Brazilian rain forest to create pasture land for cows, the cows were not to blame, but the people behind the bulldozers (incidentally, it is not the drivers, but the people who made the decision to raze the rain forest for greater profit).

To return to the story, once Dr Jekyll drank a solution that he himself had concocted, he became Mr Hyde. He killed and raped but above all, he could always return as Dr Jekyll and appear as a gentleman of class.

There are those who dream of ownership through whatever means possible; perhaps to own land sufficient to house a small army, command a business empire, possess countless wealth or live in the highest of high lifestyles. All of these may be the dream of a great number of people in the world. The question is: Will the dreamers who finally turn their dreams into reality be Dr Jekyll, or will they become Mr Hyde? There is a simple answer to the question: fortunately, we do have more Dr Jekylls in this world than Mr Hydes, otherwise, one would wonder how any of us would be able to survive Mr Hyde's merciless killing. There is another question which should also be addressed: How much ownership should individuals have, even the Dr Jekylls of the world?

The essence of capitalistic ideology suggests that it is a natural tendency for individuals who are in the position to make decisions and act on the accumulation of capital to continue the corporate expansion. Moreover, the whole idea of entrepreneurship is built on the essence of the pursuit of opportunities. It would be difficult, if not impossible for individuals who are in the marketplace to resist the temptation of the presence of opportunity. Therefore, there is nothing wrong with the accumulation of capital, corporate expansion or the creation of wealth for the individual. The question remains whether this adds value to society. Just how much ownership is considered to be justifiable, when the world has so little resources to satisfy the needs of so many? The only answer in the capitalist world is that we must trust that man will be reasonable, be of a sound mind and have a clear conscience.

Incidentally, there is some wisdom in an old saying: If you place two gold coins close to your eyes, you will see nothing, not even the gold coins, but if you place the two coins in your hands, not only will you still have your coins, but you can also see and have the world.

Ownership: The Right to Make Decisions

The essence of ownership is to give the individual the right to make decisions.

The governor of Hong Kong publicly acknowledged his desire to exercise the sovereign right (ownership until 1997) to govern Hong Kong as he sees it during an interview with the Singapore Broadcasting Corporation on 21 January 1994. He is within his right and he is certainly behaving as the rightful owner (representing the UK) of Hong Kong. In other words, as the rightful possessor of Hong Kong he wants to make decisions for Hong Kong, and he wants to make Hong Kong more democratic before the colony returns to China. The strange thing is that if he really wants to make Hong Kong more democratic, he can do it by holding a democratic election, and let the Hong Kong people govern themselves and conduct negotiations by themselves with China. This would reduce his ownership status to mere symbolism like his superior, the Queen of England. It was suggested by one of my friends, who wishes not to reveal his identity, that the governor could be very innovative about the whole thing and appoint representatives from the loyal people of Hong Kong. On the other hand, there is little likelihood that the last governor of Hong Kong will do what my friend suggested for the simple reason that since he is the rightful owner by the Treaty of Nanking 1842, he perceives that by virtue of this ownership, he has to negotiate with China on behalf of the people of Hong Kong.

Ownership and decision making work hand in hand, and the governor of Hong Kong's determination to negotiate a better deal for Hong Kong is a case in point.

The Missing Ingredients

Today, at the tail end of the civilized twentieth century, corporate executives complain about their unmotivated employees, but there is really no one to blame but themselves for not realizing the reality of life: that people cannot be motivated to make sacrifices by being told to work for the attainment of corporate goals, and cannot extend passion and love to institutions where others have ownership and they do not. Without passion and love, people are no better than androids. The greatest damage the economists (the believers, advocators and practitioners of the firm) and accountants (the believers, advocators and practitioners of the use of the rate of return on investment under current accounting practices) have done is to make human institutions dehumanized, and the great human thing we can do is to put humanity back into the human institution, that is, to recognize ownership of those who work and contribute wealth to the institution.

Putting Humanity back into Dehumanized Institutions

Economists and accountants may deserve accolades from their supporters and advocates for making the firm entrepreneurless and separating ownership from management, but they certainly cannot escape what they have done: dehumanized human institutions. On the other hand, while behavioural scientists and management experts talk so much about how to motivate people at work, if an institution is dehumanized, how would it be possible to motivate humans, since there is no human to motivate? Therefore, if it is true that man is waiting for motivation, humanity must be returned to the dehumanized institutions first. To share ownership is therefore in effect a human thing to do for the dehumanized institutions. This is a lesson that could be learned by corporate decision makers not only today but for the future as well.

People need meaning in life as claimed by Peters and Waterman, Jr. The meaning in life is none other than giving people a share of ownership, thus acquiring the right to make decisions in the process.

8

Entrepreneurship: A Matter of Attitude and the Meaning of Life

No risk, no gain, but no risk, there is loss: the loss of opportunity and the drain of existing resources.

Creativity and the Ability to Innovate Lie Within the Individual

Corporate executives may complain about their unmotivated employees for not having the entrepreneurial drive and incentive to take initiative and make changes. The reasons are twofold: First, the economists and accountants dehumanized the corporation and made it entrepreneurless, separating management from ownership; second, it is unfortunate, but nevertheless a reality, that our corporate executives do not necessarily know people's needs. They will put up the big corporate banner and ask employees to work toward corporate goals but not trouble themselves to ask people working in the firm about their needs. Without knowing people's needs it would be difficult to provide the motivation needed to stimulate the individual's desire for creativity and innovation.

On the other hand, creativity and innovation lie within the individuals. It is their responsibility to appreciate the need for these qualities, not just to strengthen the corporation's position in the marketplace, but also in the interests of the individual and society. The essence of innovation and creativity is in fact a matter of attitude. External motivation, including those provided by corporate management, is only one aspect of the many facets of the challenge.

Ownership Revisited

The desire and need for ownership makes an excellent factor for motivation. Ownership can be perceived quite differently from the way to which we are accustomed. It can be viewed from two different perspectives, both valid, depending on our perception and understanding of the meaning of life. While the perspective may not be entirely pleasant, nevertheless it is a reality.

First, we must appreciate that we start with nothing in life and shall go with nothing. Therefore, anything that anyone owns, in effect, is temporary. On the other hand, looking at a different perspective, anything under our care, for our use or under our control that may affect others or make an impact on the environment, is our responsibility. We are in fact in ownership of the circumstances, whether it be for a matter of minutes, hours or two hundred years. As the economists have said: given a long enough time, any cost is variable, a short enough time, and everything is fixed. Similarly, given a long enough time, we are tenants, or passersby, but given a short enough time, we are all owners of the circumstances. Although there are definite differences between having an ownership for two minutes compared to two hundred years, the idea of ownership over the concern is, nevertheless, very much the same. Is it not true that we own our possessions, we own our jobs while on the job, and we own our residence during the period of occupancy, even though it is on a rental basis? The idea of ownership, as noted in an earlier chapter, is a matter of making decisions and the entitlement to the harvest. On the other hand, while entitlement to the harvest has the substance of economic benefit, it is the right of decision making that has the most far-reaching effect on the individual. To illustrate, here are two incidents, one as recent as just over a year ago.

In 1992, a building in a city on the Pacific Rim caught fire and electricity failure was the cause. The fire could have been prevented from spreading if someone had turned off the main switch on the control board. Although some of the staff were aware of the situation and knew what to do, no one attempted to do so, because they had no "operational authority" (according to the procedure). Fortunately, the fire was finally brought under control. Damage to the building was limited, and there was no loss of life nor major injuries. Real disaster was averted; however, an interesting question arose from the incident: why did no one make the discretionary decision to turn off the switch?

The incident emphasizes the issue of ownership reflected in the need for an individual to make a timely discretionary decision. Ownership under the circumstances was not a matter of the individual owning shares in the company, rather it was the willingness to assume a proprietary role (I am in charge of the situation), make a decision and act upon it: to turn off the switch and to prevent the fire from spreading. If someone did turn off the switch, what would the consequences be? As in all entrepreneurial (ownership) situations, it is a question of risks and rewards.

We do not need a behavioural scientist to analyze the mind of the individual who decided to turn off the switch. It was not a question of risks or rewards, but a matter of making an immediate decision and acting upon it. Almost without doubt the person who turned off the switch was not concerned about risks or rewards, but it was to terminate the fire and prevent it from spreading. As Mr Spock (in "Star Trek") used to say: "It is the logical thing to do." Therefore, it is also a logical thing to assume that ownership and making discretionary decisions is what entrepreneurship is all about. The risks or rewards, of course, may be a concern but they only come afterwards. The rewards to the individual might be receiving a citation, cash award, promotion, or simply a pat on the back. But what were the risks? The person might be warned not to act without authority in the future, and in a worst case scenario, this might result in job loss. But none of these risks or rewards were in the mind of the individual who decided to act for the simple reason of terminating the fire.

The second situation in a sealed beam lamp factory of a multinational electric company in North America plays counterpoint to the "fire case". This time an individual took the proprietary position by making a decision in the interest of the company and people in particular as if he was in full command of the ownership position. It happened in the early 1970s, when mass labour unrest caused widespread action against the employers, including strikes, walkouts, and of course endless negotiations. More often than not, even though negotiations were supposedly based on good faith, both labour and management were merely telling each other to listen to what each (the management or labour) had to say and no one seemed to show any desire to really listen to the other's story.

Among the casualties of the labour dispute were the auto makers. All the auto workers were on strike and no one seemed to know when it would end.

The plant manager of the sealed beam lamp manufacturer had to make a difficult decision (his plant was not on strike) as the customers (the auto makers) were in the midst of the labour dispute. There were no substantial sales, no large orders coming in and the factory was stockpiling its production without knowing when the operation could be normalized. As the plant manager, he was responsible (as a profit centre) for his divisional profit performance, and for a period of three months, it was very poor: over-stocked, over-production, a drain of head office investment to the plant, negative ROI, rising costs, falling sales, cash flow and suppliers' pressure building up. All in all, every symptom meant a decision had to be made. The options were to scale down, lay off employees and continue to operate with normal shifts, or to shut down the plant, retaining only the administrative staff and essential personnel in the plant. In accordance with good management principles, the best course of action under the circumstances was a gradual scaling down of operations, reduction of programmed costs (cost escapable by managerial decision), stabilization of stockpile, and of course, laying off people. The manager had already received the red flag signal from the controller's office about his "below expected level performance".

Finally, a decision was made. The decision was not to scale down the operation, but to continue to stay on course as specified in the plant budget (in all matters except, of course, sales). The basis for the plant manager's decision was quite simple: he could not possibly see himself ordering a massive layoff. The plant had approximately 1,000 employees, including more than 70 per cent female workers, many of whom were single mothers whose pay cheques were needed to put food on the table and meet their mortgage payments. The layoff would undoubtedly cause excessive hardship to them and their families as well as the community since more than 40 per cent of the community's economy depended on the normal operation of the plant. Moreover, instead of scaling down the operation, at his own discretion, he made the decision to rent local warehousing facilities to stockpile additional lamps produced during the strike period. This was at personal risk, as his job could be at stake, but he made an ownership decision. He told his superior (the general manager) who questioned him about his unwillingness to scale down the operation that: "The company gave me this plant to run and this is how I want to run it." He was not thinking about risks or rewards; his concern was the employees and the customers (once the strike was over, the customers would immediately need supplies). The shareholders' expected rate of return on investment, if any, was probably the last consideration on his list.

Seven or eight weeks later, the auto strike was over, the plant was in a position to provide immediate replenishment for their needs, and the plant, of course, returned to its normal state of performance. The plant manager was rewarded by a promotion from plant manager to general manager in charge of manufacturing operations of the company.

The Essence of Entrepreneurship is Making Proprietary Decisions

Both cases demonstrate that the essence of entrepreneurship is not merely confined to individuals owning their own businesses. Entrepreneurship is decision making. In essence, we are all entrepreneurs, owners of our possessions and with the right to make proprietary decisions. The real surprise is that despite claiming to have dynamically provided business education to our future business persons with respect to making business decisions, little has been learned about making proprietary decisions. Teaching individuals how to reduce and eliminate risks is part of business education, but what about making decisions with risks never being part of the consideration?

We need entrepreneurs, not in the sense that everyone must own their own businesses, but entrepreneurial persons in every walk of life to build a new order: the entrepreneurial world, where everyone contributes, innovates and creates, for the purpose of creating wealth (more than just money) and adding value to society. Above all, an entrepreneurial order is vital to save the earth, our life support, homes for ourselves, our children and our grandchildren. The question is: How?

We cannot help but wonder about our economic progress to date which is in fact not an accomplishment but a rip-off from our silent partners, and from our children and grandchildren's right to live. If not, why have our statisticians invented the idea of reporting GDP (GNP), while not mentioning a word on DLS, the Depletion of Life Support, or indexing the DNR or Drain of Natural Resources?

Developing Entrepreneurial Persons Building an Entrepreneurial World, and Criteria of Success

At the beginning of an MBA entrepreneurship class (1993) at the Nanyang Technological University, Singapore, students discussed at great length the usefulness of learning about entrepreneurial attributes from research findings and how to be a successful entrepreneur in the conventional sense (to be in business). The first question from the group was about the meaning of success. Was Howard Hughes successful? The answer was yes and no. Yes, he reached a phenomenal level of business and financial success, but he was personally miserable and isolated himself from the rest of the world. This raises another question: Who or what is successful and in what?

Success is not a matter of having three wives, or being rich enough to be able to make an "indecent proposal" to rent someone's wife for one night. A Nobel prize winner may be successful in achieving the highest recognition in the world for the discovery of a cure for AIDS, but might not be happy about devoting too much time to research and not having enough time for family. A successful businessman may have all the wealth in the world at his command but may sadly neglect his son in the process. To allay his guilt over this neglect, he spoils him with every materialistic thing possible, and eventually passes control of his entire estate to his son, with assets sufficient to pay off the US national deficit. But the son is such a spoiled individual that he wastes all his father's "hard earned money" and gets into drugs and various other illegal operations. He is caught, tried and then sentenced to hang as a result. The once rich man would be left with nothing but his son's grave to cry over: is he a success?

Individuals have their own criteria of success. The author's daughter, a physician, once told him: "Dad, I don't believe it. When I talk and give consultation to my patients, I realized that whatever I say to my patients is what you told me all the time when I was a child." To the author, that is success. It is not money, inheritance, or glorification, but a simple sharing of thought and appreciation between two human beings. Success is therefore in the individual's perception of what success means to him. There is no absolute medium through which success can be measured that suits everyone's expectations. Our researchers may never want to verify that the greatest success and satisfaction to an individual does not come from profitable (financial gains) undertakings, but endeavours not for profit. It is difficult to convince profiteers and stockbrokers of this wisdom.

As the MBA group got into discussions about the usefulness of learning entrepreneurial attributes, it was felt that the whole exercise was nothing but a glorification of some financially successful individuals. It was like a show and tell class and had very little meaning for the individual. As a result, a critical twofold question was raised:

1. If we are lacking some or all of these entrepreneurial attributes, what should we do? Does it mean we are not entrepreneurs?
2. If we possess the same attributes as described in the texts or research papers, do we still qualify as entrepreneurs, even though we are not as successful (measured financially, or business-wise) as those glorified financially successful individuals?

As in any discussion, there was no consensus, but the group felt strongly that entrepreneurs are learners, and they are fast, eager and willing to learn in the presence of needs. The answer to the second part of the question was obvious; all people have different notions about their own success.

To learn, develop, enhance and nurture essentials that will develop an individual's attitude, attributes, and skills toward creation and innovation are challenges. We are obligated to undertake this challenge, if creating wealth and adding value to develop individuals as entrepreneurial persons will in turn help build our perceived entrepreneurial world.

Adopting an Entrepreneurial Attitude and a Habit to Learn

Attitude is how we deal with realities. We all look at things differently; some of us tend to be negative and resist change, and others tend always to be positive. We, as entrepreneurs, should always look at things positively. There are at least three aspects to being positive: be positive, positive reinforcement, and the attitude toward risk.

Be Positive

Energy is positive and creative; it will only become negative, or destructive if it is abused. Similarly, human beings are essentially positive and will only become negative once they have experienced hardship, unpleasant situations, discomfort, and/or had their security and safety threatened. Whether this can be empirically tested is immaterial; what matters is how it can be used to create a positive attitude.

To be positive means always to view things positively. Here again, the Chinese have something to say about how to perceive things positively. Most of us are familiar with the example of a bottle filled with water. When the bottle is full, then it is "full", but if it is half filled, there are two ways to view it: it could mean the bottle is half empty which is negative, but it would be positive if it is viewed as half full.

In addition to viewing things positively, this attitude also helps individuals to develop an entrepreneurial mentality of perceiving problems differently. Problems are problems but as the author has said many times before, there are perceived opportunities in every problem situation. For example, a horseback rider who fails in his first attempt at a jump can learn as much about himself and his horse from discovering why he failed as if he had succeeded the first time around. A failure in business provides learning opportunities to increase the possibilities of future success. The author recalls a story where a person was confronted by his personal enemy at gunpoint, and appeared to be relieved rather than afraid. He said to his enemy: "I am sick and tired of running from you. Shoot me; you will free me from this miserable existence." Strangely enough, his enemy did not shoot him. Instead, they started to communicate (by whatever means), and in the end walked away together as if they were long lost friends.

Positive Reinforcement

Positive reinforcement is an entrepreneurial attitude applying to situations to encourage initiative and to be supportive in the presence of unfortunate happenings, including errors, solecisms, blunders and other unpleasant incidents.

As normal human behaviour, people who take the trouble to take an initiative would expect a positive response rather than be confronted with negative remarks such as:

"You will never make it."
"Your whole idea is nothing but a dream."
"You don't have the experience."
"Forget it, I heard that before."

A positive response simply suggests that instead of saying "no" and making nasty remarks about the initiative, respond with a "yes" to the idea, even though the idea is not new or implementable, but still worthwhile considering. It should be noted that there is no such thing as failure, unless there is a beginning and completion (end) to a process. Although an initiative has to be scrutinized and analyzed for feasibility for implementation, a rejection can only be made after this process.

A supportive attitude toward unfortunate happenings suggests that individuals should have an understanding attitude with a desire to help overcome difficult hurdles. If, on the other hand, either body language or expressed anger and displeasure over the incident provokes the individual responsible, this could block communication, making a bad situation worse. To illustrate, consider the following situation.

A brought a project proposal to B, who worked in the same institution. His colleagues recognized B as being very knowledgeable and sought his consultation and evaluation of the proposal. B viewed the proposal and indicated that the project had been attempted by others who failed, and in his opinion, it was a "no go". A insisted and convinced B, who admired A's determination. B made a few suggestions and gave a qualified "yes" to A. A proceeded with the project but failed. A then went to B's office and said to him: "B, the project couldn't get off the ground." Under the circumstances, B could have responded: "I told you it wouldn't work!"

If B had done that, A could have reacted unfavourably: "Don't rub it in, I know I was wrong." A could have walked out of B's office, and that could have been the end of the communication, ending their good working relationship. On the other hand, B could respond positively, reinforcing his entrepreneurial initiative (taking the initiative and assuming the risks) by saying: "Not necessarily, let's look at the result. We can learn from this and reshape your original proposal. If all parties agree, I am with you and we shall try it again." B could also say: "The experience and information we get from this project can be used for another project. Let's look at the possibility of using the information and result for project 'X'. If you think I can be of any help to you, just let me know, I will join you on this. That is, if you want me."

Attitude Toward Risks

A risk is not a risk itself, it was once said: "There is nothing to fear but fear itself." The truth is that when a person is in the risk situation, there is no concern for risk but to struggle to get out of the risk. Risk increases an individual's strength and capability to deal with crises and discoveries.

It is seldom noted by people that the fear of risk and perception of risk are always greater than the risk itself. In business, there is a common expression: "No risk, no gain". There is also a risk avoidance attitude with an expression: "No risk, no loss". The first is true, but the latter is false, since if there is no risk, there is a loss of opportunity. Moreover, while consumption must continue, no risk will drain existing resources, and this is loss itself. To an entrepreneur, risks are challenges. Mountain climbers, skiers, swimmers and even the bicycle riders are viewed as risk-takers. In fact, we are all risk-takers. Some take greater risks, others take moderate risks, but there is no such thing as no risk in human endeavours. To take risks is a fact of life, a necessary process for discoveries and achievements. It would be a meaningless exercise just to realize that entrepreneurs (business) are risk-takers, but adopting a positive attitude toward risks and developing an ability to deal with risks are the essence of entrepreneurship development, and a never ending challenge to mankind now and in the future.

Developing a Learning Habit

Life is a learning process, and even people with no desire to learn, are still learning as they learn "not to learn".

We learn in formalized situations, and if we so wish, from informal situations as well. In the author's life, there have been many great learning experiences. One such experience was watching two blind men, one black and one white, walking with their white canes along a street (in the area of Bathurst Street and St. Clair Avenue in Toronto, Canada) hand in hand. They walked, talked and laughed together, without concern for the colour of their skin, age, appearance, or religion. It was such a beautiful sight, making the author learn to appreciate the meaning of a truly beautiful human relationship. Perhaps others did as well, if they could appreciate this beautiful reality. At that time, there was also another thought in the author's mind: Would we have a better world if we were all blind?

As a teacher for many years, the author has always considered that he has learned from his students as much as he has taught them. As the author frequently told his students: When a teacher learns from his students, he gets paid and when the students learn from their teacher, the students do not get paid, the teacher does.

The ability and willingness to learn is a great gift from nature. The more the individual learns the more creative the individual will be. This is not just the learning of technologies and skills that are essential to enable us to find a place in society. It is not just learning from schools, but also learning from animals, learning from our environment, and the most rewarding experience that the author can suggest is learning to know and appreciate people and the differences in people, and as a result, to benefit from each other.

Developing Entrepreneurial Attributes

Virtually all entrepreneurial attributes advocated by most researchers are common to all human beings. Everybody in the world under normal conditions has self-confidence, and when the situation requires, everyone can be and is a leader in his or her field. Every person in the world wishes to achieve his or her own goals or objectives. Of course, some are more strongly motivated than others, especially in the more creative and innovative activities. All individuals are essentially willing learners, but some can learn faster than others. Similarly, entrepreneurial attributes can also be developed by everyone, provided the individuals are willing. The willingness to learn is closely related to the "responsiveness to suggestions and criticism" attribute and can be developed and enhanced. The following are a few suggestions with respect to the enhancement of selected entrepreneurial attributes advanced by countless researchers during the past four or five decades.

Self-confidence

Self-confidence is a mindset. Confidence comes with success, as one success leads to another success. The more successful experiences an individual possesses, the more the individual will feel confident about himself. Therefore, it is not self-confidence that one should strive for first, but success. Self-confidence will come after success.

In the self-enhancement process, an individual can develop and enhance personal success by:

1. Establishing a criterion and the meaning of success. A criterion for success can be as simple as exercising the discipline of practising weight control. Once the weight is under control, it is definitely a success. Another example of a simple criterion for success is meeting deadlines. We all have the feeling of success if deadlines are met. Once a series of successes has been experienced, an individual will have developed greater self-confidence.

2. Establishing realistic and attainable goals. To establish realistic and attainable goals is a statement of motherhood, and has been said by many people countless times. Nevertheless, it is an effective way to experience the meaning of success. It is obvious that if a goal is unattainable, success will also be unattainable. An attainable goal of a new venture must give consideration to strategic fit including personal resources, capability (within the given constraints), environmental variables and other factors.

3. Success should be measurable. Non-measurable success does not sustain self-confidence. Measurable success does. Experiences of measurable success is a self-confidence enhancer for the individual.

Creativity

We are naturally creative. Development of the individual's need for creativity is not probable, but definitely possible.

The principal function of the entrepreneur is to carry out new combinations of means of production. Under the circumstances, the key phrase for creativity is "new combinations". Artists are, of course, creative individuals. Their desire to create encompasses both form and colour. The three primary colours, red, blue and yellow (they are called primary because no other colours can be combined to make red, blue or yellow) can create countless colours; for example, red and yellow make orange, red and blue make purple and to combine orange and purple will create another colour. The artist perceives the need to create meaning in his paintings and through the use of colours.

Similar to the artist's creation of colours, any individual can develop his creative desire by experimenting with new combinations, or by simply attempting to do things differently. All of these could be done at work, while managing a business, at home, or in the laboratory. Once the creative desire becomes part of the individual, creativity will be a continuous process. It is the same as the energy flow that benefits us on an ongoing basis.

Perseverance and Determination

During the Second World War, a message was passed along the Allied front lines as a form of encouragement. The message was: "Don't quit five minutes before midnight." This message puts perseverance in its proper perspective.

Perseverance is an individual's dedication to the continuing pursuit of an ongoing course of action despite hindrances, obstacles or frustrations. It is an attribute that individuals can enhance and develop, thus becoming a base on which future success can be built.

When perseverance leads to success, this encourages greater perseverance. Just as in athletics, perseverance must be built up. While you might not be able to do fifty push-ups today, if you can do one today, and make it your goal to do it every day, and one more each week (surely an attainable goal) within a year you will be doing those fifty push-ups. It is the determination to accomplish your goal which ultimately leads to success.

This prescription may appear as if the author is practising the profession of a psychologist without a licence. However, it is based on the author's involvement with students in different parts of the world over thirty years. The same suggestions were given to countless students who sought consultation because they were unable to cope with term work, examinations, personal or family pressures. The suggestions worked for them, and in a few cases, actually prevented an attempted suicide. Remember: "Don't quit five minutes before midnight."

Flexibility

Flexibility is a natural asset for all human beings. It is the ability to adapt to unpleasant or difficult situations. The idea of changing ourselves to fit into the environment or changing the environment to suit our needs illustrates the flexibility of human nature. Flexibility leads to survival, to better relations with others and is a pathway to success.

As with other attributes, flexibility can be learned and developed by individuals. The following few suggestions are to help individuals develop more flexible attributes both in working with people and making decisions:

1. Develop options, with a good grasp of these options.
2. Develop a clear understanding that any joint human endeavour should be to the interest and benefit of both parties. When thinking of benefiting from the endeavour, you must also think of the others involved who should benefit in the same way as you.
3. Develop a willing attitude to accept alternative or optional solutions. Make decisions with a clear understanding of the nature of these options, what they mean to you and the others involved.
4. Adopt a flexible attitude and mentality of uninformed optimism. In the world we live in today, it does not really matter how advanced our information is because there is really no such thing as perfect information. An entrepreneurial-minded individual must always be optimistic about the outcome of an opportunity. An uninformed optimistic mentality provides an individual with a flexible attitude which is more acceptable to others.

Leadership

Leadership comes as a birthright. Given the opportunity everyone can be a leader in his own field. People in positions of power are leaders in their responsibility for others; skilled individuals are leaders where skills are concerned, a knowledgeable individual is a leader in information, and an entrepreneur who has created his own business and is committed to managing the business would be the leader of the business. A leader is not someone who stands on top of the mountain and tells everyone beneath that "I am the leader". A leader must lead his followers. A leader without followers is not a leader, while an ordinary person with followers is in effect, a leader.

A true leader is a person who can have followers, work with others, and provide services where services are needed. A leader need not head anything but must appreciate interpersonal relations and be someone others are willing to identify with. In the human environment, a leader is always a person, not a superior human being or a god.

If the meaning of leadership is properly appreciated, then leadership means possessing leadership qualities, and is not necessarily leadership in the conventional sense. Leadership qualities can be developed through individual efforts. Individuals with leadership qualities are always leaders whatever their titles or official status.

There are also other commonly acknowledged entrepreneurial attributes. It is not important to single out successful business persons and ask them to define entrepreneurial attributes that contributed to their success. It should not be surprising that the answer would be: hard work, perseverance, self-confidence, initiative, willingness to take risks, dynamism, flexibility, ambition and resourcefulness. What do all these mean? Most people would think: "I have the same attributes, why do I still punch the time clock (or work nine-to-five, or have my own business, and work sixteen hours a day) and still can't make a decent living for myself and my family?" The fact is that all those attributes mean nothing to an individual unless the individual appreciates that:

1. Practically every individual possesses all these attributes, but the individual must learn how to apply them when and where the situations render themselves to be applied.
2. All these attributes can be developed and strengthened, and the individuals must take every opportunity to strengthen and develop these attributes into personal assets.

The author, by his own admission, is a quick decision maker. This dynamism attribute was not learned from textbooks, successful entrepreneurs or great leaders, but when the author was facing a life and death situation at the age of eleven as a third class refugee (the author defines first class as those organized by church groups, second class as refugees with families, so naturally, the author was a third class refugee, since he was not from a church-organized group and had no family). It was during the early stages of the Japanese invasion of China, and gunfire had destroyed the author's family and the families of many others. Alone and running for his life with gunfire at his back, other refugees and retreating soldiers from all directions, he had no idea where to go. Crying for help was useless; there was nowhere to stand, or rest, and no food. The author was pushed, kicked and hurled abuse by others (better class refugees and soldiers) who were yelling: "Get away!

Move! Move!" Everybody was on the run but no one seemed to know where to run.

As a third class refugee, the author had to make decisions all the time: Where to go? Who to follow? There was no time to think nor gather relevant information; just make decisions and run. Decisions were made, not in a matter of days, hours or minutes, but instantly. The author decided to follow the retreating soldiers. Had he not done so, one may wonder who would have written this book and told his story? Incidentally, this was what happened: The author was picked up by a colonel in a retreating field gun regiment of the army, and settled temporarily in the second line (for re-grouping and re-training). The colonel made him a staff sergeant, and assigned him a casual function of writing reports and preparing the payroll for his regiment. He was dumped when the troop returned to the front line some six months later. Once again, the author was a third class refugee at the advanced age of twelve.

Learning and Developing Entrepreneurial Skills

Over the years, there have been endless arguments as to whether entrepreneurship (more appropriately, business entrepreneurship) can be taught, and whether there are "left brain" and "right brain" solutions. Teachers tend to say, "Yes, it can be taught, and should be taught." However, there are also others insisting that entrepreneurship cannot be taught even though entrepreneurial skills can. As a teacher, the author would have to say, "Yes, entrepreneurship can be taught but not the mindset or spirit." Nevertheless, it can be cultivated, nurtured and developed, while skills certainly can be taught or developed.

Some commonly acknowledged entrepreneurial skills include communication skills, interpersonal skills, networking skills, negotiation skills, analytical skills and planning skills. More can be added to the list but six should be enough.

Communication Skills

Everyone can communicate, but communicating effectively, meaningfully and pleasantly is another matter. It is not an overstatement to say that most of our problems are caused by our inability to communicate. The USA and the former Soviet Union never communicated effectively and meaningfully during the entire Cold War. If we could communicate effectively and meaningfully with one another, we would finally have peace on earth, happiness and prosperity for all.

The following are communication skills we should develop:

1. Be a good listener. Listening is communicating. To listen is to allow maximum elbow room for the other person's freedom of expression. To have the desire and capacity to listen to others is an excellent communication skill. It is effective and meaningful, but how can you improve it? The answer is simple: be sincere, and listen sincerely as if you do not wish to miss a word. Listen to whatever the other person has to tell even if the same thing has been said before. One frequent response from unconcerned listeners to the person repeating the story about his interesting adventures is: "Oh! You told me that before." The fact is any person of sound mind would eventually realize this and stop the "torture" before going too far by saying: "Oh, I told you that before." If the torture is not too painful, encourage the storyteller to finish the story by saying: "Please go on, it's interesting." The exercise is a simple matter to allow others to feel free to express themselves.

2. Be caring, interested and responsive. As a listener, it is vital to impress the speaker with your reception of his words. Listening should come with favourable facial expressions, showing a genuine interest in what the speaker has to say.

3. Smile. The smile must be from the heart. Smile genuinely, not professionally.

There are also a few don'ts in communication skills:

1. Don't use excessive body language. Body language often suggests displeasure toward the communicator. Even pleasant body language such as hugging, laughing and waving hands can often be wrongly perceived. Unfriendly body language can hinder effective communication, block communication and even terminate communication. Communication is not just what one says or does, but how one is perceived.

2. Don't use sarcastic language. Statements such as: "I am sure you can do better than this", or "You have made enough mistakes for the day, you can go home now" should be avoided.

3. Don't scream, or raise your voice. Screaming or raising your voice during normal conversation suggests that the communicator does not know how to communicate effectively with a normal tone of voice or a normal expression. This invites a screaming match, and can effectively terminate proper communication, inducing hostility and creating misunderstandings.

4. Don't interrupt information flow. Always allow the other person to communicate and complete the delivery of his ideas, arguments and suggestions.

5. Don't change the topic. If it is necessary to change the topic, end the previous topic in a satisfactory manner and then introduce the new topic at the appropriate time.

6. Don't allow any obstacles in between communicators. Any obstacle can block the communication, and to be effective, if it is at all possible, communication should occur face to face.

Last, but not least, it is always desirable to communicate in a pleasant environment. In the event a verbal communication is not possible, learn from a great lady, Mrs Jannie Tay of Singapore. When she found that she could not get her idea through to her business partner, her husband, the CEO of the Hour Glass, she wrote letters. The author had a similar experience when communicating with his youngest daughter. He found that a written letter was more effective than face to face communication. In other words, communication means different things under different circumstances and language is only one form of communication. Explore other means to communicate if verbal communication becomes ineffective or creates misunderstanding.

Interpersonal Skills

Most of the communication skills and positive attitudes are applicable to interpersonal relations. An effective, good, sincere communicator with a positive attitude probably has good interpersonal skills. There are other areas of interpersonal skills development.

1. Learn how to give as well as how to receive. Some people know how to give, and others how to receive. An entrepreneurial person should know both. Giving need not involve money or anything of material substance. Caring and sharing are all part of giving and receiving. The bottom line of how to give and receive is a matter of sincere appreciation and gratification of expression extended between and among individuals.

2. Approachability. Approachability is a simple gesture to make others feel that you are available if they are in need. "My door is always open" is good, but not enough; a more effective interpersonal skill requires a mutual feeling of: "My office has no walls."

3. Building bridges not walls. The idea of building bridges and not walls suggests an individual should find a way to reach others or

make it possible for them to do the same (building a bridge to allow others to cross). On the other hand, two individuals face to face can even have walls between them: a deliberate attempt to ignore the other's presence, harsh remarks, unfriendly body lauguage and, among other things, refusing to communicate (such as not returning telephone calls) are cases in point.

Interpersonal skills can always be developed. The key to developing interpersonal skills is to interact with others on any occasion and in any place with sincerity and concern for others. Some people gain the skill in their childhood (through play and interaction with other children and/ or adults), while others may not appreciate its need even when entering into adulthood, whether at work, at social gatherings, at church functions or in the marketplace.

Negotiation Skills

In one airline's inflight magazine, an international consulting firm was attempting to make a point with a simple advertisement (by including a photograph of a person with a successful look, no smile, looking straight ahead, and quite serious) by saying: "In business, you don't get what you want, you get what you negotiate." The interesting thing is that many of these important skills are not part of learning; individuals have to learn them by themselves. There is another popular saying in business: "In business, everything is negotiable, the only difference is the price." Is this true? No wonder someone had the imagination to make up the story in the movie *Indecent Proposal* that with a million dollars, one could negotiate for someone's wife for one night.

Negotiation is a skill, but it is not a skill with the intention of making a killing. Good negotiation skills must be supported by sincerity, good faith and the intention that the end result will be fruitful to both parties. A sincere negotiation will not have one party beginning the negotiation from the floor (the bottom), and the other from the sky. It is rather a reasonable approach to assume the other's sincerity until proven other-wise. A friend of the author once told him to watch out when entering into negotiations with "some" people in Hong Kong. He said: "At the end of the negotiation with "some" people, when shaking hands, make sure that they haven't taken your arm away with them." If this is true, it is certainly not the entrepreneurial type of negotiation for persons to take someone's arm away as part of the deal.

It has to be noted that there is no certain set of skills that can be programmed. A skilful negotiator should always be prepared, able to steer negotiation constructively, and always ready to make a reasonable offer. There are also a few simple guidelines in addition to the above that could be observed:

○ Carefully study all documentation relating to the matter to be negotiated. Consult experts, if there is anything you do not understand.
○ Be punctual.
○ Do not volunteer information unnecessarily.
○ Keep personal feelings out of the negotiation.
○ Remain friendly, even if a deal does not go through.

Analytical Skills

Analytical skills refer to an individual's ability to assemble available information and make immediate use of it. The skill for analysis is no different from the formal learning of the problem solving model. It is the one so popularly used in business management teaching materials, and includes defining the problem, searching for information, analyzing information, selecting alternatives, evaluating alternatives and making a decision. A similar approach can also be used in skills development, except they can be simplified where appropriate.

Most analytical skills involve the use of quantitative methods. It has to be noted that statistical information is all historical, whereas accounting information is also historical, but more often than not, includes a prediction of future events, such as budgets, forecasts and projections. All historical information must be used with care, since what has happened before, may not be the same in the future, and any predictions based on historical information has built-in deficiencies, because it includes past inefficiencies into the forecast.

There is no short and sweet guide to developing analytical skills, but it is possible to acquire a few simple techniques to enhance an individual's analytical ability. Those who have no particular interest in quantitative information can learn to accept and appreciate its power by simply using them in accordance with their needs. For example, percentage expression is more meaningful than figures, and to correlate one figure with another is always fun. In any event, if quantitative analysis is such a drain on an individual's intellectual capacity, it can always be done by computers, or simply by having someone else do the analysis. Be sure, the person doing the analysis should also be prepared to explain the analysis and show how it applies to the particular situation. To play with figures is always fun even if the outcome is wrong, but to know that it is wrong is a learning experience.

Analysing human character, ability and capability is not as simple as quantitative analysis. A curriculum vitae will tell part of the story; a reference check and proof of the diploma or degree are part of the input available for analysis. There is also such a thing as gut feeling. Someone once said about analyzing people: "When you see a sincere person, you know it." What else can we say?

Planning Skills

To develop an individual's planning skills, that individual first has to learn to like planning. It is not just to plan everything in the head, but to do a plan in a more formal sense, either by writing the plan down, enter it into the computer, or recording it on tape. Without formalization, it can easily get lost if everything is in one's head. Everybody plans, except some plans are more formal than others.

This book does not teach people how to do a business plan, but to develop planning skills as part of entrepreneurial skills development. Planning skills include:

- Learning to like planning and developing a planning habit
- Always putting the plan in writing, taping it in an audio tape recorder or storing it into a computer
- Learning to appreciate that a formal plan is better than an informal plan, and an informal plan is better than no plan at all
- Remembering that a good plan always has the users of the plan in mind

As with most skills, these are repetitive in nature, and repetition helps to improve planning skills and developing planning habits. The only caveat is that one must not be a slave to the plan. As in the bicycle story, planning for the sake of the plan is not any better than the man carrying his bicycle to work instead of riding it.

Nurturing the Entrepreneurial Spirit

To a large extent, human beings are habitual animals; once they get into a habit, everything will go on as usual. We have certain ways of doing things, such as going to a restaurant and requesting for the same table. We have a certain hour to get up and even have a certain way of brushing our teeth. The point is, to nurture the entrepreneurial spirit is a matter of getting into the habit of being creative and innovative and always being ready for action. What has been described earlier are essential types of habitual behaviour that will help to nurture and enhance the entrepreneurial drive.

To nurture the entrepreneurial spirit is a function of both the individual, home and society. At the individual level, one must have a clear understanding that the spirit is within the individual; it has to be self-cultivated and nurtured. Thus it can flourish through all endeavours.

Entrepreneurship: The Meaning of Life

Peters and Waterman Jr (1982) suggest that we must give meaning to life. Life is energy, and energy is dynamic; so is humanity. The dynamism of entrepreneurship is a drive within ourselves, inducing and pushing us to explore, discover, invent, use different combinations either in goods, or ideas, to create and innovate. All this is the meaning of life. The principle of entrepreneurship can be applied as readily in non-commercial as in commercial ventures, in economic endeavours and in human relations. In other words, the entrepreneurial drive may spur the start up of a new venture, but the spirit of entrepreneurship may lead an individual to much larger life experiences. It is the desire of the individual to create and innovate that created this world. What is important is twofold: we need the entrepreneurial spirit at all times to create wealth for ourselves individually or collectively as a group, but this must also add value to our society. It is in the value adding context that we are obligated to extend our care and passion to our environment since which we are inextricably a part of it.

9

Passion, Love and Sharing

It is the energy in us that drives us to create. It is the passion we possess that makes us to love what we create, and it is the love for what we create that makes us want to share with others.

Motherhood

In North America, when someone states the obvious with respect to the common good, some people will say: "Here they go again, supporting motherhood." This means "if you have something original to say, say it, but don't give us this motherhood stuff".

Passion, love and sharing in the context of entrepreneurship is not just motherhood, it underlies the meaning of creation through commitment between individuals, and from humanity as a whole to the

150

environment and our planet. The energy in us drives us to create, the passion we possess makes us love what we create, and it is the love for what we create that makes us want to share with others.

The author's wife, Flora, joined him on his visit to Singapore. After settling in an apartment provided by the university, away from children, relatives, friends and the familiar environment of home, suddenly she was alone while the author went to his office at the university. The empty rooms and the absolute silence completely distorted her emotional balance, and she told the author: "I can't stand this absolute isolation. I scream and cry, but this gives me no relief. Many times I have wanted to go back home by myself, but I know I can't do that to you. There are two options open to me: to go home is one, and the other is to do something before going crazy." Out of desperation, she used a pencil and a few sheets of paper and started to make a few simple drawings of whatever came to mind. She showed her drawings to the author, and with his encouragement, she began looking for a school or somebody to teach her painting but to no avail. Being in a strange place she did not know where to go; it was like looking for a needle in a haystack. She bought a book entitled *How to Paint with Acrylics*, and after going through the book, she started painting as well as experimenting with the mixing of colours. As she said when she started to paint, "It was like being in the middle of a deep lake without knowing how to swim. I had to grab any object that came to me and hang on to it." So she painted and painted, from simple objects to creative scenery, from beautiful skies to brilliantly coloured forests, from white bark birch trees to green pastures, from silvery snow to spring glories, from lily ponds to creeks and waterfalls. She created her own scenery and expressed her own imagination. Without going to school or receiving any instruction from anyone, she earned her name as an "artist". After less than two years of "artistic life", one of her paintings is hanging on the receiving room wall at the home of the High Commissioner for Canada in Singapore, as well as in the homes of many private collectors. More often than not, at two or three in the morning, she and the author will sit in front of her paintings, sharing deep passion for and love of her work. Something else was also emerging: she wanted to share her creation, not just with the author, but also with her friends and everyone who appreciates art.

Her friends love her work, and admire her drive and dedication to develop her talents without any outside assistance. She has shared her experience with them and without knowing how, has helped them develop their need for creation. Today, a number of her friends have expressed a desire to take up painting, and at least three of them have officially enrolled in the Nanyang Academy of Fine Arts, one of them actually resigning from a paid job to join the group.

This is a clear illustration of how energy drives an individual to create, how passion and love extended to the creation, and in particular, how through passion and love, the willingness to share creation with others is developed.

As human beings we are creative by nature. Our inherent assets of passion and love bind humanity together as a whole. This passion and love spur on the need for sharing. Therefore, by nature we are all willing givers. Some give their lives to their religious beliefs, some for their country, and some for their causes. While some give their lives, most commonly, love is given through creation, sharing their harvest and, most importantly, sharing their ownership.

The Sharing of the Harvest and Ownership

While entrepreneurship and the issue of ownership have far wider connotations than just in business, economic entities and, more specifically, businesses are matters of great concern these days. Therefore, this chapter will be devoted mostly to the humanity aspects of business operations. In short, it describes how to put humanity back into dehumanized institutions.

The Sharing of the Harvest

Sharing the harvest is a simple expression of appreciation. Some harvest-sharing ideas are included in formal distribution systems and are in fact implemented throughout the world. Other ideas may be in the stage of incubation; these include the idea of profit sharing, year end bonuses and other forms of incentives. In other words, sharing is part of profit distribution rather than deductions from revenue.

Among the various sharings, the following two are commonly acknowledged practices:

1. Direct profit sharing. The firm allocates a certain percentage of the profit to distribute to employees, to be added to their December pay cheque, or in a separate cheque indicated as a year end bonus.
2. Profit allocation to match employees' pension contribution. This method attracts more senior employees to stay on. There are various stipulations. For example, there could be a certain time limit imposed on the withdrawal of the pension such as, if individuals have less than five years of contribution, they may only withdraw their own contributions with or without interest. After five years,

they may withdraw the entire amount including the company's contribution. The program works well to attract the employee's commitment to the firm for a longer period of employment. As such, the older an employee is, the better the pension benefit will be. The pension fund per employee increases if more people withdraw their pension contribution after less than five years of service.

The Recognition of Intellectual Property

The recognition of the intellectual assets of the individual is directly associated with a recent drive among people who advocate intrepreneurship. It is an extension of the profit centre concept, attempting to address the failure to motivate corporate managers to strive for the attainment of corporate goals. The intrepreneurship concept refers to "entrepreneurs inside the corporation, people who implement new ideas inside established companies and who, though employed in a corporate position are nevertheless given the freedom and incentives to create and market their own ideas" (Haskins and Williams, cited in Gibb, 1990). For example, an inventor in a company is awarded a percentage of the ownership of the invention (much the same as the percentage of sales revenue to an author of a book). In essence, such recognition applies only to the sharing of the revenue (or profit) aspect of ownership. The inventor seldom has the entitlement of making decisions unless the patent is granted to the individual and not to the company.

Ownership: The Meaning in Our Lives

What is the meaning in our lives? This is a soul-searching question, but the answer rests with each individual. All of us, at times, find the meaning in our lives, but more often than not, it eludes us, changing under different circumstances and at different times.

During the 1994 Chinese New Year, the author was in Taipei and visited a Chinese temple. There he witnessed an impressive display of human expression. It was a wonderful example of giving, an inspirational reflection on the meaning in our lives which we experience yet which often goes unnoticed.

It was early in the morning on the first day of Chinese New Year. It looked as if the entire population was moving, inch by inch, to the same destination: to the temple that housed the "Deity of Brotherhood" (Guan Gong, a hero in the period of the Three Kingdoms). As everyone proceeded to the altar to pay their respects to the deity, they joined a series of queues. There were long lines outside the central court of the temple leading to a side building with people collecting money for a local hospital. The queues were so long that the author had to wait for at least one hour before reaching the cashier to give his contribution. The contributions made by worshippers were not merely hundreds of (New Taiwan) dollars, but thousands and thousands of dollars. It was not merely the sight of a big crowd making a contribution to a worthy cause; they appeared to have found the meaning in their lives — they were not buying a one-way ticket to heaven, rather they were queuing up to give for the good of others.

Although it is difficult to find an appropriate expression of universal meaning in our lives, on the other hand, if there is anything that resembles the idea of universality it would be ownership. In the business world, it is ownership that gives people the right to make decisions and entitlement to residuals.

The Sharing of Ownership

For large corporations, giving ownership to key executives has been a long time practice, and equity participation is part of the package to attract and retain their top performers and key position executives. There is one particular equity participation which, although it has only a short history, is worth noting. It works for this particular company, a giant auto parts maker that started up with a small plant, and has now grown to be a billion-dollar business.

This particular company gives plant managers the opportunity to purchase company shares at a price well below market value. Ownership stays with the plant manager as long as he holds a position in the company. When a manager decides to leave the company, the shares must be sold to his successor. In the event of the death of a particular manager, the company will redeem his shares which would subsequently be made available to other plant managers at an appropriate time. The scheme is designed to keep the shares held by its plant managers within the firm, preventing them from flowing into the market.

Both the sharing of ownership and harvest are designed to motivate employees to develop a passion for their company, a sense of belonging and pride in having a piece of the action in the company. Many of these schemes work well, but there are also pitfalls, particularly, in smaller firms and family businesses. The principal shareholders of several companies went to the author's consultancy and expressed their concern about the loss of total control of the firm, and a dilution of profits as the firm's value appreciated over time. On the other hand, sharing ownership in smaller entrepreneur-managed companies, with no resources for a comprehensive employee development programme, nor benefit package to retain good employees, may be an effective incentive to reduce high employee turnover often prevalent in smaller companies.

In an unpublished study (Kay et al., 1994), thirty-nine Singapore entrepreneurs (as classified by researchers) responded to a 150-item questionnaire. This was followed by interviews with twelve of them. All twelve held the positive view that equity (ownership) sharing was beneficial for employee motivation and/or soliciting commitment to the company. A similar question was addressed to approximately 120 entrepreneurs in Canada (Kao, 1980), who also favoured the sharing of ownership with their employees (equity participation), with a number of them actually involved in sharing schemes. There were concerns about the possible erosion of control. Nevertheless, respondents felt that the scheme provided better motivation and commitment to the company.

There are various means of sharing ownership. The equity incentive plan permits employees to purchase company shares at an affordable price, often below the actual market value of the shares, or a price reflecting a range traded in the stock market. Simply giving out shares to loyal employees as an incentive for their good performance and loyalty to the company is another way of sharing ownership. The shares sold or given to employees could be common shares (ordinary shares), or preferred shares with varied options (voting powers, participative, accumulative versus non-accumulative, convertible, etc.). The same arrangements are also in practice among partnership firms and firms held by sole proprietors. Under the circumstances, when admitting a new partner (this is a form of sharing ownership, and may take the form of a general partnership or a limited partnership), there would be a change in the legal structure of the firm, and consequently, a reorganization is required. The change might be either from a sole proprietorship to a partnership, or a limited partnership, or may involve dissolving the old partnership and forming another one that includes the new partner or partners.

Through the author's consulting experiences and interaction with smaller firms over the past few decades, he has often found a general reluctance to become involved in ownership sharing schemes. For unlisted companies, issuing shares to employees can be a source of frustration frequently involving the following concerns:

1. What is the right number of shares to be awarded to employees?
2. What if shares held by employees are sold to parties whom I do not wish to be involved in my business?
3. What happens if they request my company's books be audited? (In Canada, any limited liability company's book should be audited.

But if the company does not directly solicit public financing, then it has no obligation to provide financial information to outsiders, if the shareholders indicate in writing that the company's books of account do not require a public accountant's audit. On the other hand, minority shareholders, more often than not, do not exercise the right to request that the company's books be audited by a public accountant.)

4. It is difficult to administer an ownership sharing plan.
5. If the plan is implemented for certain employees only (for example, division managers), it may induce dissatisfaction among other employees and build up their resentment toward the company because of the unfair treatment.

Under these circumstances, many smaller firms prefer to offer other forms of financial rewards.

Spin-offs and the Incubator Concept

Spin-offs and the incubator concept are used by a number of large corporations such as AT & T to nurture new products and develop technologies they believe to be worth exploring. The spin-off incubator concept is very much the same as the business incubation concept, which has been in practice in many countries (Canada, US, South Africa and others) except that a number of small new ventures are housed under one roof, sharing common facilities. The spin-off incubator concept differs from the business incubation concept in ownership, the process of nurturing and the spin-off from the parent company reflecting these differences are summarized in Table 9.1.

In summary, in the corporate spin-off incubator concept individuals are encouraged to come forward with ideas, and then an internal group within the corporation evaluates the ideas to determine whether they are marketable. If they are, a mini-company is established. The idea is funded and the originators are given the opportunity to take their brain-child and run it. For this reason, it is also called intrepreneurship; in other words, entrepreneurship incubated, nurtured and developed within the corporate structure. The strength of the spin-off incubator approach to create new ventures is that it allows individuals to experiment with their ideas within a large organization where they have a certain amount of leeway in terms of time, money and other forms of resources which would not be available otherwise. On the other hand, it should be noted, that so long as the parent company is the majority shareholder of the new corporation, and within the general management structure, subject

Table 9.1
Business incubation

	Commercial approach under business development concept	Corporate approach spin-off from the parent company
Incubating	Independent entrepreneurs	Technical employees or division managers
Plant	Individual enterprise as a tenant under a contract	Provided as part of the parent company under R & D or divisional budget
Management	Independent	Under the corporate general management structure
Decision making	Individual entrepreneur/ manager	Individual manager within budgetary constraints or by the approval of a superior
Resources	Individual entrepreneur arranges all financial and other resource requirements	Provided by the corporation (parent company)
Management services	Provided by the incubator's management on a fee basis	Provided by the parent company
Ownership	Entrepreneur owns the company. If outsiders are involved, it could be in a partnership or a limited liability. In this case, shareholders hold the ownership. More often than not, the entrepreneur holds majority shares	The parent company owns the company. Once a new company is formed, the investor (the technical employee and/or division manager) will likely be awarded partial ownership of the new company
Risks	Borne by the entrepreneur and other investors	Financial risk is assumed by the parent company in stages of incubating and nurturing. Once a new company is formed, it will be the shareholders of the new corporation who assume the risk limited to their equity participation
Operational environment	In the marketplace	In the marketplace with protection provided by the corporation
Level of autonomy	100%	Independent, but subject to corporate control

to corporate control, then it is really an extension of the profit centre concept as noted in an earlier chapter. On the other hand, if the tendency of the new corporation swings toward the formation of a joint venture, then assuming that the parent company is not the major shareholder (assume the parent company holds 30 per cent, outsiders 40 per cent, the inventor or division manager 30 per cent) this will be a new corporation under a new management. Therefore, it is the entrepreneurial drive within the corporation that creates the new corporation. It is a spin-off process, and the new corporation will not be within the parent corporate structure.

Incidentally, a similar practice had also been implemented in the UK in what may best be described as a spin-off to new venture creations. The fundamental difference between the particular spin-off approach in the UK to the incubator approach is that the creation of the new venture within the corporation structure is not caused by new ideas. It is caused by divisions within the corporate structure which have failed to perform up to the corporate standards, but could be profitable, if the structure is changed. Under the circumstances, the division manager may be approached to take the division out of the corporation and form a new company, giving him partial ownership to run it. However, a close examination of both the spin-off approach and incubator approach within the corporate structure shows that it is still very much the same as the profit centre concept which has been in the marketplace for quite some time.

A Stakeholder Approach to Business Ownership Challenge

Entrepreneurship is a way of life, and the seeds of entrepreneurship lie in all of us. New ideas and their creations are the basic purpose of our lives. What we need is the ability to make decisions, and the opportunity to make life more meaningful through increased involvement in the wealth creation and value adding process. In business, this has been a simple working model which has been used for quite some time: the model allows individuals in the workplace to acquire ownership through their own efforts.

It is not difficult to share ownership in the corporate structure. To do so, all the individual needs is money. With money, one may purchase shareholdings as long as they are available in the marketplace and the price is right. Sharing ownership with individuals (employees) in the firm whose shares are not traded in the stock market is not as easy as it appears; more often than not, it is a painful process. This is simply because ownership is treated as if it is an untouchable "sacred cow". In many people's minds, they are not only unwilling to share the harvest, but also the important issue of decision making. A frequently noted remark states: Sharing ownership is no different from allowing strangers in my house telling me how to run my household. On the other hand, there is an open admission in organizations that employees tend to be more loyal if they have a stake in the organization.

In the working environment, passion, care, love and creative ideas are the result of having a stake in the organization. Individuals tend to be reluctant to devote more than normal working requirement efforts, and rarely take the initiative to offer creative ideas and to be creative and innovative if they are merely employees of the organization. Let us look at the motherhood concept one more time; to entitle an individual to a stake in the organization is a commitment from an individual (decision maker) to another individual. It is the idea of promoting the common good in the interest of the organization, the individual and society as well.

The proposed stakeholder approach to business ownership is an option that can be considered to activate the entrepreneurial spirit of the individual, and hence, improve economic performance in the process.

The model may be described as follows. Assume a large corporation has a paid-up capital of $800,000,000, shares are held by various individuals and institutions, the shares are publicly traded and the expected return on shareholders' investment is 20 per cent, the annual dividend is about $10 per share, and the price per share with moderate fluctuation is about $100. Further assume the annual sales is about $4,000,000,000. Figure 9.1 shows a simple operating statement.

It is further assumed that the earnings and dividend payments are very much in line with the market trends. The $80,000,000 residual represents various individuals' contribution to the organization, not just the shareholders' capital at work. The non-capital contribution to the residual is defined as the stake.

Assuming that Stake Corporation's decision makers (most likely the Board of Directors) decided that employees' contribution should be recognized, but with a number of stipulations:

1. Of the residual, 10 per cent should be allocated for employees' participation.
2. An employee is defined as a person in contractual agreement with the Board of Directors, and not a member of the Board.
3. An allotment of shares of the stake will be made available for employees' participation.
4. The price of the stake share will be determined by the Board, but no less than 5 per cent, and no more than 20 per cent of the equity share price traded in the stock market.

Figure 9.1

Stake Corporation
Operating Statement
31 March 2xxx

Sales	$3,000,000,000
Cost of sales	1,880,000,000
Gross margin	1,120,000,000
Less: Commercial, administration and financial costs	800,000,000
Net profit before tax	320,000,000
Less: Taxes	160,000,000
Net financial income	$ 160,000,000

Common shares fully paid = 8,000,000 shares at approximately
$100 per share = $800,000,000

ROI = $160,000,000 / 800,000,000 = 20%

Dividends paid = $10 per share = $10 x 8,000,000 = $80,000,000

Residual = Net financial income – Dividend = $80,000,000

---

5. Stake shares are entitled to the same dividends as determined by the Board.

6. Total amount of stake shares must not exceed 10 per cent of the total equity shares traded in the market.

7. Stakeholders may elect one member to sit on the Board either as a voting member (representing all stakeholders) or non-voting member of the Board.

8. A stakeholder must surrender his stakeholdings to the company if he ceases to be a member of the company. The price of the share may be determined by the Board, but at no less than 10 per cent of the equity share price traded in the stock market, or the price paid at the time of purchase of the stake shares.

9. Stakeholders may attend the company's shareholders' meeting, but with no voting privileges.

10. A stakeholder may not be a member of the union. If in the event a stakeholder wishes to withdraw his participation, he may do so by surrendering his shares to the company at the original subscription price paid by the employee. He may then join the union.

11. The maximum number of shares purchased by any one individual may be limited by the Board.

12. Additional stake shares may be issued on an annual basis.

13. The stakeholdings must be redeemed by the company at a price of less than 10 per cent of equity share price traded in the stock market. If so desired, the redemption amount may be added to the company's employees' pension plan upon retirement, and the company may work out an annuity as it deems appropriate for the individual.

14. The stake participation plan should not cause any great equity share price fluctuation. If, in any event, it affects the equity share price, the Board reserves the right to make necessary adjustments in order to maintain the company's share price at a reasonable level so it will not discourage investors' investment interest in the company.

15. Employees may elect a payroll deduction plan to purchase stake shares.

16. At the time of retirement, the stakeholder may elect to redeem the shares in cash (at the market value of equity shares traded in the stock market) or the shares may be left with the company on an annuity basis amortized until the retiree reaches the age of ninety-one. Should the retiree die before age ninety-one, the balance will be added to the estate.

Figure 9.2 is an illustration of the equity section of the company's balance sheet before and after the implementation of the plan.

Figure 9.2

	BEFORE	AFTER
Stake Corporation		
Equity Statement		
As of 31 March 2xxx		
Common shares		
8,000,000 shares @ $100	$800,000,000	$800,000,000
Operational residual	80,000,000	80,000,000
Total	$880,000,000	
Issuance of 80,000 stake shares @ $10		800,000
Total		$880,800,000

Equity share book value before issuing stake shares
= $880,000,000/8,000,000 = $110.00

Share book value after issuing stake shares
= $880,800,000/8,080,000 = $109.01

Accordingly, there will be an erosion of the equity share book value of approximately $1 per share which may be a disincentive to investors because of employees' participation. Share trading value may decrease as a result.

The proposal is intended to provide an incentive for individuals in the firm to be able to identify themselves with the firm, to develop the caring, passion and love for the firm and stimulate their inherent desires to be creative and innovative. Ownership in the organization is the key ingredient that induces creativity. On the other hand, what happens if the idea of the stakeholder approach to shared ownership or any other ownership sharing plan is unsuitable or unacceptable to the decision makers of the organization?

Let's Put Humanity Back into the Dehumanized Institutions

The economists and accountants must share the responsibility for making business an entrepreneurless entity, and dehumanizing it by separating management from ownership. In economics, a firm is entrepreneurless; in accounting, machines, computers, buildings and even toilet paper (as supplies) are classified as assets, but not human beings. None of these assets is subject to motivation, but human beings are. Is it possible to put humanity back into the dehumanized institutions and expect them to be motivated? The answer is obvious, so why not put humanity back into the dehumanized institutions? How should it be done? It cannot be done by modifying human resources management policy, waving banners, shouting slogans, or bringing out the motherhood concept that everyone must work for the attainment of corporate goals. Nonetheless, there might be people once again bringing out their ideas for dealing with the challenge: "If I have money, can I use money to buy humanity?" Can it be possible?

There are no perfect solutions. Therefore, no attempt will be made to search for a perfect solution, but only for a workable one. It is workable because it is just a matter of developing an appreciative attitude toward people, by using and putting people first and attempting to provide a human environment for human endeavours. The stake ownership proposal outlined earlier is by no means revolutionary. It is based on the existing industrial structure, and among other things, the assumption that people can be motivated to make sacrifices, if they can only find meaning in their lives. It should be noted that in an entrepreneurial corporation, everyone in the corporation is an entrepreneur by right, except the investors of the corporation, since the prime objective for their investment is profit. Investors have a good name in society. Why should they change their honourable status to the level of the hard-working entrepreneurs' group? What the proposal attempts to do is to rediscover the human energy in humanity and put it back into the dehumanized institutions. First, let us start with the corporate entrepreneurship.

The Riddle of Corporate Entrepreneurship

For whatever reasons a large number of corporate executives have convinced themselves that in order to activate human resources in the organization and to stimulate them to be creative, thus giving the firm a competitive edge in the marketplace, they must make a great attempt to restore the entrepreneurial spirit. The inducement of intrepreneurship is one example and while not every situation justifies the creation of another profit centre or mini-company, attempts have been made to modify the corporate strategy to adopt the idea of entrepreneurship by calling it "corporate entrepreneurship". The intention is noble, and some of this has, in all fairness, generated results.

Academics often attempt to gather and quantify other people's experiences, which are then brought into the classroom and with the help of the computer made into theories and concepts. Unfortunately, they usually pay too little attention to imagination, creativity and innovation. One problem is the means (research including the use of questionnaires, interviews, etc., as research methodologies) used to collect information, collate their research results and tell people: "This is what Simon says." Simon says:

> Among the 300 best managed companies, their success in maintaining the lead in the marketplace is due to their ability to create a favourable environment. This induces change and the advancement of technological sophistication, dynamism, all of which facilitate entrepreneurial activities.

What this means to other firms is anyone's guess. However, if the relevance of such findings is raised, then the researcher might say:

> I have done all I can to create an environment as described in the research findings: my company continues to pursue technological progress, make changes to deal with competitive rivalry, make regulatory developments, and explore niches away from traditional markets by embarking on new product or process development, but people in my firm still behave like dead wood, as they always have. Nevertheless, there have been some improvements. All I can say is that if they (the dead wood) were a group of "walking dead" before, they are now upgraded to "walking wounded".

What would the researchers say if they were directly challenged with the situation? They might say:

> I have told you all I can to improve efficiency and productivity and make people more creative and innovative. It still does not work. What you need is to hire a bunch of people with six fingers on their hands.

Of course, the question would then be: "Yes, I agree with everything you say, but where can I find people with six fingers?" The answer: "That is your challenge." I am sure the conversation would end right here. The riddle is that while the successful firms have found the light at the end of the tunnel, all the others are still very much in the dark. Why is that? Is entrepreneurship so sophisticated that it is the domain of only a few? The answer is "No, entrepreneurship is not unreachable, but it is within ourselves. All we need is to search inside our souls and let the spirit of entrepreneurship out into clear and clean air."

Where do we start? Let the author once more practise a profession without a licence and prescribe the "no magic medicine". The magic of "no magic medicine" for the corporate executive is simple. Do not think like the CEO of a giant corporation with net assets of US$5 billion. Think like a plain Joe or Mary on what they want in life and on the meaning of life. By doing so, you will not merely think of how to earn that rate of return on investment so that the Board will grant additional corporate shares or millions of dollars in tax free bonuses. You will think of what Mary, Joe and other individuals in the firm have on their minds and what they need. After all, in the executive corporate lifestyle, you always assumed that you were working for the company. Why not think of working with the people in your company for them and the company? Instead of asking people in the company to work to attain the goal of the company, you think of what the company can do to help individuals in the company to achieve their personal goals. Since you have always talked about goal congruence, how can we have goal congruence if there is only a one way street? If you do think so, you will throw the whole silly idea of the theory of the firm out of the window. This is a risk you would have to take if you want to practise corporate entrepreneurship. Will you risk your private executive washroom key to do this? The guarantee is you would not lose it if you do not risk it, but if you do, you might get an even bigger executive washroom key for a very big private washroom, if you need it.

Incidentally, much has been said about the need theories and the research done about people's needs. Academics and consultants have their share of excitement, and they still do. In fact, the excitement continues not only in dealing with people at work in factories and offices, but is widely used in the marketplace and consumer behaviour studies.

What is disappointing is that even though business executives know about the importance of the awareness of employees' needs and their personal goals, in practice, to care about employees' needs is still nothing more than window dressing. On the other hand, if company executives are really serious and concerned about employees' needs, why has hardly any attempt been made to find out what their personal goals and needs are? For example, why not provide a space in the job application form to invite job applicants to express what their personal goals and needs are?

How should we start? First, let us have a clear understanding that entrepreneurship is a wealth creation and value-adding process. An entrepreneur is not someone who must have his own business, and the author is not the only one who says so. According to Schumpeter, entrepreneurs are people who are creative and innovative, and are not only those who are managers of small businesses. More importantly, they are those creating jobs and preparing society for change. Entrepreneurship lies in us. It has to be thoroughly filtered all the way into everyone's mind.

There are no limits to the cultivation, nurture and development of entrepreneurship. It could start as early as in the cradle, or as late as one minute before the end of the journey of life. So, for businesses, if the decision makers are willing, change can take place at any time.

The following are a few suggestions that might not be universally aggreeable, but cost very little to try.

1. Changing attitudes toward people

Do not assume that every job applicant is applying just for the money, or a position in the company where he or she will work to attain the goal of the company. People work for many different reasons. Therefore, it is a sensible thing to find out their personal goals first. To do so, the company can simply provide a space in the job application form for the applicant to tell the company about his personal goals and ask how the company can help to achieve them. Although not everyone is clear on personal goals, it is a start. For example, one individual may say: "I want to realize my dream to be the CEO of my own company, to be a cancer researcher, or alternatively to be elevated with the growth of the company."

2. Find out whether the individual knows how to achieve personal goals

After finding every individual's personal goals, it would be very helpful to know whether he knows how to achieve those personal goals. If so, resources should be made available (perhaps a consultative process) for him to use if in need. On the other hand, if he does not know how to achieve his personal goals, assist him to map out a strategy to achieve it.

3. Develop an entrepreneurial attitude in the organization

Entrepreneurs tend to emphasize active experimentation over reflective observations; unfortunately, throughout the educational system, and in particular, in business schools, the reverse is usually practised, using the reflection of experiences in order to build theories. To catch up and bridge the teaching style, the organization should respond to pragmatic demands for relevance and the application of knowledge and work experience. The working individual should integrate previous scholarly learning and experiences in life to apply to the real work situation. The managerial role in the firm is not supervision nor direction, but belongs to a resource person who is self-directed, who gains insight into the reality and wisdom of learning and applies it to personal conceptions of reality. Working is learning and experiencing, but not a repetitive exercise, otherwise, it can be computerized.

4. To create a self-assured decision making environment

Everyone makes decisions, including making the decision of not making a decision. But it is the strange reality that, as a rule, people tend to make decisions for others, including personal affairs; for example, what to eat, whom to marry (in some families, marriage is not a simple individual decision), when to sleep, how to sleep, how many children should we have, how to dress, how to behave, and in fact, everything imaginable. There is always someone who will tell us what to do, even what to think, although the person may not know what we are thinking. Consequently, this could make some of us feel that we just do not know how to make decisions. Otherwise, how could Shakespeare have written such a beautiful profundity: "to be or not to be, that is the question"? Decisions, decisions, what are we to do if we do not know how to make decisions?

The trouble with making decisions for others is, it makes one wonder how this world was ever built? Obviously our parents have told us what to do ever since we were born, teachers tell us what to do (if you do not obey, you may get lousy marks), consultants tell us what to do (how else can their fees be justified?), professionals tell us what to do (do they have any choice? It is part of the profession), and of course, the highest level of telling people what to do is in the working environment where we are told to follow the yellow brick road of systems and procedures. As a result, we really do not know how to make decisions, if such decisions are outside of the procedure or system, or if there is no one to tell us how to make that decision.

Entrepreneurship is making decisions and acting on it. If in an organization, individuals are unable to make discretionary decisions, then everything is for the birds. Should this be the case, our economists would be happy to know that the firm is not only entrepreneurless, but also humanless. How to encourage and develop an individual's decision making capability? These are questions of competence, confidence and leadership. By the way, this sounds as if the author is flogging a dead horse of entrepreneurial attributes, but the fact is, he is attempting to bring the dead horse back to life, and develop entrepreneurial attributes and individual values and skills that will give individuals the decision making capacity needed. Here again, the author is trying to tell people what to do. Why not? This is why you are reading this book, is it not?

5. Developing entrepreneurial attributes

Some of the author's colleagues said that there are at least some forty or even fifty entrepreneurial attributes, but after exhaustive studies, only about thirty-two have been noted. As these attributes have been listed by many at many different times, the author wishes to apologize to those researchers for bringing them out and not being professional enough to have them individually aknowledged. Nevertheless, should you wish to know what they are, look at the earlier chapter or in Chapter 10. Just think for a minute, if you are able to enhance and develop these attributes, do you not agree that you will surely know how to make discretionary decisions? Just as the case of the fire incident in the building mentioned in Chapter 8, where no one acted on his own accord to turn off the power switch and prevent the fire. The question then is who will do the job to develop these attributes for the individuals. Instead of referring to six-fingered people, you might wish to know about the following:

> Some years ago, an emperor wished to know something about economics, so he called fifteen of his ministers and told them to write a book about economics. In no time at all, fifteen beautifully bound volumes on economics were presented to the emperor, but he became very angry and told the ministers: "Who do you think you are? I don't have the time to read all this." So he ordered ten of the fifteen to be beheaded on the spot, and said to the rest: "This will teach you a lesson not to fool around with me, be sure to do your job right." The five retreated, and later brought back one volume and pledged: "Your High and All Mighty, we have exhausted our brains to

construct this volume that will tell you everything about economics." The emperor was even angrier, and without saying another word, told the guards to have four of the five beheaded. The last one went white with fear but he retreated and later came back and knelt before the emperor in tears and said: "Your High and All Mighty, here is a book on economics." The book was very thin, containing one sentence in one page, and it read: "Economics is: there is no such thing as a free meal."

Here you go, if you want to have corporate entrepreneurship you will have to work for it since there is no such thing as a free meal. Moreover, corporate executives ought to know that there is no entrepreneurship in an entity if the entity is entrepreneurless.

It should be noted that to develop the individual's attributes is by far a more effective approach than to tell the individuals how to make discretionary decisions. As the story goes: "If you give a person a fish, it would only last him one meal, but if you teach him how to fish, this will last him a lifetime. If you develop his sense of conservation and teach him how to fish responsibly, he will have the capacity to fish for life and, much more important, the commitment to conservation, so there will be plenty of fish for him and for future generations."

6. Developing the individual's personal values

A corporation has its own corporate values and every individual has his own values. We all have different values: religious values, family values and societal values. These values stay with us, guiding us throughout our lives. They are learned and internalized, reflecting the process of socialization into a culture, a corporate culture or an organizational culture. As a personal value system is a powerful force in life, if there is any meaning to an organization, these individuals' value systems should be developed and integrated into the value system of the corporation. Corporate values work best from the bottom up, not necessarily from the top down.

7. Developing the individual's entrepreneurial skills

Skills are personal assets. Better equipped entrepreneurial skills increase the individual's competence and confidence in making discretionary decisions. It really does not matter whether an individual is running a business, working in a laboratory or is on the road to negotiate a deal on behalf of a company. Various skills such as communication, interpersonal and analytical skills have already been discussed in Chapter 8. Skills development is both the responsibility of the individual and the corporation, since a skilful individual is of benefit to both the individual and the firm. Unlike entrepreneurial attributes, personal values rise solely out of the individual's desire to develop them. While external factors do contribute, it is the individual's personal efforts that count. For example, what can one do to encourage an individual to take risks, if he thinks and behaves like an individual who lives in a plastic bubble? Skills, on the other hand, can be taught and that is the reason why a large number of people advocate that the formal educational system should assume responsibility for entrepreneurship skills development. Figure 9.3 is an illustration of an entrepreneurship development model for corporations.

Figure 9.3
An entrepreneurship development model for corporations:
an energy circle approach to entrepreneurship development

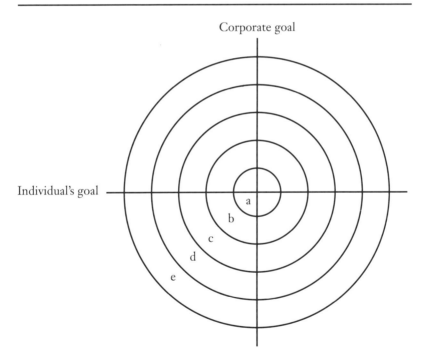

a. Individual
b. Individual's personal values
c. Individual's entrepreneurial attributes
d. Individual's entrepreneurial skills
e. Corporate enterprise culture

The Big Picture

Passion, love and sharing at the individual level is a commitment on the individual level to develop the individual's creativity and desire to innovate by putting humanity back into the dehumanized institutions. The big picture is that humanity as a whole must commit itself to extending its passion, love and sharing to our planet earth. To illustrate the point, for example, in the interest of conservation and preservation of fish stock, Canada's new Liberal government issued a moratorium on fishing off the Atlantic coast that cost Canada's poorest province to lose thousands of jobs. On the other hand, it would be useless, if the commercial fishing fleets from other countries such as France and Japan do not assume a moral responsibility and respect the Canadian efforts.

The United Nations' Role in Environmental Protection

There is an organization within the UN framework working for the protection of human rights, but only with a token expression on protecting the planet and the environment. As a world body created in the interest of humanity, it makes virtually no attempt to protect the vital interest of humanity, our environment. Why this is so is anyone's guess. But it is about time that this world body takes an initiative to account for environmental damages and damages done to our life support. Therefore, it is proposed that this world body establishes an environmental and planet protection office on an equal footing with the Food and Agriculture Organization, International Labour Office and Human Rights Commission. It should be charged with the responsibility of publishing research findings and everything that has to do with the environment and erosion of earth's ability to support human beings and other living creatures. This information must be further aggregated into a database accessible to every member-nation in the world. This database must be accounted for before deriving a country's GDP (Gross Domestic Product) or GNP (Gross National Product). A country whose current GNP growth rate of, say, 12 per cent may have it reduced to 1 per cent because of an index such as DLS (Depletion of Life Support) or DNR (Drain of Natural Resources) guided by the UN. In other cases, GDP could even be negative, if the aggregate of DLS and DNR is greater than GNP.

The Accountants' Role in Environment and Earth Protection

The story of profit never ends but accountants can still make the profit story more relevant to reflect the real profit, not just from the point of view of the individual firm, but the environment and the planet as well. Since our planet and the environment suffer loss as the result of making profits, profit is really no different from taking blood from a sick person. Therefore, if the UN initiates a database of environmental and planet damage, it would be the responsibility of our accounting profession to integrate it into determining profit. The challenge to our accounting profession is not a justification to clients, corporations or government but to our children. Surely, we want our children to have the right to live just as much as we do. Otherwise, we may have to take them into the grave with us. Is that what we want?

The responsibility to save our earth and the environment lies not with the environmentalists whose efforts only induce government intervention, but with the business persons who have the greatest responsibility of all. It is the accountants' professional and moral obligation to tell them that what they call making profit is really akin to taking blood from an already bleeding planet and its environment. Only the business persons can help the environment, not the environmentalists, nor governments. It is the business persons' responsibility to ensure that if we make a profit, the environment and planet should make a profit as well, or suffer the least loss. While entrepreneurship is a wealth creation and value added process, improper business conduct without concern for the environment, gives an individual business person more money in the pocket, but certainly does not add value to the society.

10

Entrepreneurship: It is Not a Highway to Heaven, but a Vehicle to Economic Freedom

Once you buy a lottery ticket, you are in the hands of God, if you create a business of your own, you and God work together as partners.

Is There a Highway to Heaven?

Inasmuch as we have heard so much about heaven, it is a mystery whether there really is a heaven. In the author's childhood days, it was said that heaven was above the clouds; the coming of the airplanes flying above the clouds exposed that story. Children in China have heard untold stories about heaven, including the story of the "Journey to the West", but we now know that heaven is nowhere on earth. Astronauts Neil Armstrong and several others have landed on the moon, so we know that the moon is not part of heaven. We have landed vehicles on

172

Mars, and perhaps on other planets in the not too distant future. Heaven is not there either. Then, where is heaven? Religious persons may tell us there is a heaven, and if you do this, and not that, you will be in heaven one of these days (assuming that you have to leave this world first). Still, they cannot show us where heaven is or give us the slightest description about what heaven really is. Certainly, even if there is a heaven, we do not know how to get there.

Others may claim that heaven or hell is what we make of our time right here on earth. If you are rich, you are in heaven. Whether or not this is a relevant claim is questionable because "richness" is a relative term. A person could control an entire nation's wealth, but is that person rich? We do not really know; if we did, no one would have said: "There is something to be said about being a simple person."

Entrepreneurship is certainly not a highway to heaven; it is not even a guarantee that you will be rich. However, by being creative and innovative, one can earn economic freedom, whether by going into business, or working in a business or other organizations. As the seeds of entrepreneurship lie in us, by cultivating and nurturing what is already in ourselves, the seeds of entrepreneurship will germinate, sprout and grow to be trees. They will not only provide shade for ourselves, but for others as well. This is the meaning of life within ourselves that will take us to economic freedom.

Although entrepreneurship is not the domain of profit making businesses only, today the world is shifting toward the western style of market economy. Thus it would be most meaningful to the majority of us to be more focused on the challenge of ownership in business through the creation and the development of business enterprises. Under these circumstances, the balance of this chapter will be devoted to the creation and development of business enterprises. In fact, more often than not, it is this form of entrepreneurship that has led people to economic freedom, whether it be under the western style of market economy, or a market economy under a socialist system.

Entrepreneurship: A Vehicle to Economic Freedom

Many a promotion currently on the market tells people that by attending some seminar (and incidentally paying a few hundred dollars) you will be provided with a road map to the kingdom of riches. One of the most common schemes involves buying and selling real estate. Although most schemes are a waste of time, there is nevertheless some wisdom in the idea. Dr Sun Yat-Sen's (the founder of the Republic of China) land tax theory implied clearly that the scarcity of land, high demand and social progress would augment land price. Anything in the market system can have a period of depression in price, which could fall so low that it would disappear from the market (caused by a shift in demand for example), but seldom, if ever, does this include land prices. This is partly because of increase in population and partly because of development and social progress. Land cannot be replaced by other products but only by new locations, therefore, its price will go up all the time. Under the current situation (1994), China is the prime target of the land purchase fever, even though its property market has already peaked. Many individuals are eyeing other parts of the Far East, such as Vietnam and Burma, while some have a mind to venture into land profiteering in India. However, this form of venture is not an entrepreneurial undertaking. Land development, which creates wealth and adds value, is an entrepreneurial undertaking, but purchasing land for speculation is at best a questionable money making scheme. In such a case, a land speculator is a profiteer and not an entrepreneur. Hence, the real estate business will not be part of this discussion, even though one can be a profiteer through land speculation, and also be an entrepreneur if one engages in creative and innovative value adding endeavours.

The Process of New Venture Creation

There are many publications which tell the stories of successful entrepreneurs (their endeavours have added value to society as well as created wealth for themselves). The recent publication *Stepping Out*, by Chan Kwok Bun and Claire Chiang, vividly illustrates how Chinese entrepreneurs have made their fortunes through hard work, good human skills and among other things, the possession of many entrepreneurial attributes. The author was involved in the development of Canada's TVOntario's "Front Runners" series which tells about nine successful Canadian entrepreneurs (such as Three Buoys Houseboat Vacations Ltd) and their recent successes in business (unfortunately, two of the nine are now out of business). The *Official Guide to Taiwan* (Vol. 21, No. 2, 1994) tells a story about a young entrepreneur, Jack C. N. Chen, one of the great success stories of Taiwan. Twenty-one years ago, Jack went to work for a yacht builder. Six years later, the company was failing and Jack was able to buy it. Today, Bluewater Yacht Builders is one of the leaders of the industry. In McMullan and Long's *Developing New Ventures* (1990), a host of successful entrepreneurs, both dead and alive, are paraded through the book, including Henry Ford, Morita, Matthew Boulton, Mary Kay Ash, Meng Teh-ho, Alfred Krupp, and of course, Wozniak and Jobs and the "Apple Story". It should be noted that in the case of Meng Teh-ho, he was successful despite the political environment. It was at a time when the hardline Chinese Communists did not particularly favour entrepreneurship. This is a telling argument that entrepreneurship is a way of life no matter what the political system is. The stories tell us how those individuals, prompted by the entrepreneurial drive, have made themselves rich and even famous (in print), and achieved economic freedom.

If these stories do not impress you, just look at the nations on the Pacific Rim. Singapore has no land space and absolutely no natural resources, yet through collective and individual entrepreneurial efforts the people of Singapore created a great nation. Malaysia, Thailand, Taiwan, Indonesia, Korea, and of course, China are viewed by westerners as developing countries; many of them fall under Canada's CIDA (Canadian International Development Agency) programme or similar programmes from other industrial countries. Yet they are now the fastest growing economies in the world, and much of their growing success is attributable to individuals who aspire to a life free from poverty. Entrepreneurship is the key to the economic freedom they crave.

There is no assurance that you will be as rich as Henry Ford or Mary Kay Ash, but owning your own business will give you something you would never otherwise experience: the satisfaction of making your own decisions, charting your own course and accepting the consequences. However, rather than plunging directly into unknown territory, exposing yourself to a formal learning environment will increase your chances of success, and most important of all, eliminate some unnecessary frustrations. There is so much to be learned, most of which are skills, skills that have been noted in Chapters 8 and 9.

Before Starting up

To make life simple, the author, based on his experience in consultation, teaching and his own business endeavours, has developed a simple model (see Figure 10.1) to affirm an individual's attitude for embarking on the start-up of a new venture under the assumption that the individual already has the proven product or service and is ready to take needed action.

The first part of the model (top left box) is all about entrepreneurial attributes. The idea is to examine these attributes and do what you can to enhance what you already possess. For example, being responsive to suggestions and criticism simply suggests that you should listen to what others have to say, but make your own decisions about actions (to go or not to go). The skill of identifying market niches is a matter of finding a hole in the market, that is, find a need for a certain product or service that is not available, or is available, but inadequately served.

Figure 10.1

Entrepreneurship application: New venture development model

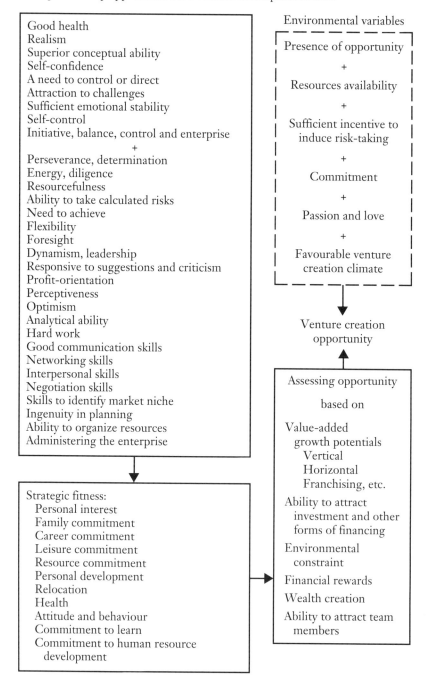

The next part (bottom left box) is essentially a process of self-assessment. In the old days, the reason for starting a business could be a matter of survival. Today, with so many new entrepreneurs coming from positions in large organizations, the reason for starting a business may be that they wish to be better off, or simply wish to be able to make independent decisions for the future. The bottom right hand box is the assessment of opportunity, that is, will they fit into the opportunity while staying within their personal profile and desires. Finally, inter-action with environmental variables is the box on the top right hand side of the model.

Making Decisions

The entire venture creation procedure consists of making decisions and acting upon them. There is no need to restrict yourself to an artificial routine such as: first step, second step or step-by-step approach to venture creation, but there are priorities. All priorities can be ranked in order of necessity and should be flexible and, if necessary, changed. If anything should have top priority among all other priorities, it is to get ready and go.

Get Ready and Go

1. Look for a market niche. Once a niche is found, assess its feasibility immediately and make a decision to pursue this niche.
2. Make every attempt to acquire needed resources, both financial and human.
3. Once resources appear to be available, enter into negotiations with other parties (this could involve inviting an investor, partner or financier) and make decisions on how a deal may be structured, and on the contract to be agreed upon while keeping in mind that all of these will affect the organization of the firm. For example, one must consider the degree of investor involvement, share distribution, the legal form of the organization, partner status and work commitment in the firm and above all, the protection of equity.
4. Prepare a simple business plan. If the plan is for the venture founder's own use, it can be in any form or style. On the other hand, if it is for the purposes of other users (such as for investors or bankers), the plan must be prepared with this use in mind. A plan is a consolidation of thoughts, and a way to assemble resources that

can be used to guide actions. Therefore, it is always better to have a plan, as even the worse plan is still better than no plan at all.

Implementing the Plan

A plan is useless if it is not going to be implemented. However, a plan need not reflect reality completely, and it can always be modified when more information is available. For example, a sales forecast for new ventures at best is nothing more than just an educated guess (see top part of Table 10.1). If, on the other hand, the actual first three months' sales were far below the original forecast, the forecast could then be revised in accordance with reality (see bottom part of Table 10.1).

Table 10.1

Guess Corporation Pte Ltd **Sales and Revenue Forecast** **For the period January – December 2xxx**												
$'000	Jan	Feb	Mar	Apr	May	Jun	Jul	Aug	Sep	Oct	Nov	Dec
Sales	100	120	120	130	140	150	160	180	200	250	250	300
Sales and Revenue (Actual and Forecast)												
Sales												
Actual	50	40	50									
Forecast				60	70	80	90	100	120	200	200	250

The revised forecast consists of the first three months' actual sales and a forecast for the balance of the year. This will serve as a simple guide and it also illustrates how a plan works for the individual.

Decision to Start up a New Enterprise, Buying an Existing Firm or Becoming a Franchisee

People with a new product, a new service or other marketable ideas, particularly those with limited immediate cash, should consider starting up their own business. Starting the business at home is a sensible choice, but it is necessary to observe the local by-laws, zoning regulations and neighbourhood attitudes toward operating a business in a residential area. In most cases, to start up a new business, the venture founder should consider the following when assessing the opportunity:

1. Capital requirement. Low capital requirement normally means low entry barriers both for yourself and others. In other words, if the business has great success potential, consideration should be given to the protection of the product (service) through means such as sufficient differentiation, unique design, or patenting, at least in the home country and in major countries where the product will be sold.

2. Financial returns. Without sufficient knowledge of the future, it is necessary for the venture founder to do some simple financial estimates (see Figure 10.2):

   (a) Estimate the amount of total investment required to start up the business.

   (b) Estimate the full cost of the product. The full cost means the owner/entrepreneur's personal sacrifice must be recognized (remuneration) as well as the opportunity for capital investment.

   (c) Work out a simple cash flow.

   (d) Distinguish between fixed and variable costs.

   (e) Do a simple profit-cost-volume analysis, including:

      ○ cash break-even
      ○ break-even without taking into consideration the owner/ entrepreneur's full remuneration
      ○ break-even

Figure 10.2

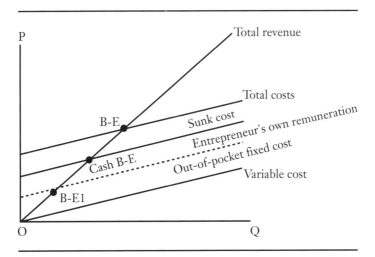

(f) Calculate operational profit.

(g) Calculate return on capital investment.

3. Operating leverage. High fixed cost requires high volume sales, but after break-even, it will generate greater profit. However, it must be recognized that no cost is absolutely fixed. If the volume is high enough, for example, certain fixed costs have to be increased, because capacity has to increase to accommodate the high volume.

4. Potential of the business. There is the question of possible expansion, once the business is successfully launched.

The preceding simple guide is also applicable to acquiring an existing business. Of course, there are additional considerations and some of those considerations are common to all purchase situations. For example, price, the continuation of existing management, and above all if the business premise is rented, the length of the existing lease and the conditions for renewal. There are a few other areas that should also be observed:

1. Purchase price. Price is one thing, payment is another, but in most cases, terms can be negotiated. For example, cash plus debenture, term payment or other forms of arrangement are in the interest of the buyer as well as the seller in respect of cash flow, financial planning and, above all, the matter of control. All of this should be considered and, if possible, negotiated on the best terms.

2. Financing. The seller may wish to stay on as a minority shareholder; otherwise, venture capitalists could be considered or other investors invited to join in on the purchase. Under the circumstances, it is necessary to enter into a more sophisticated negotiation in terms of "deal structure", including shares of ownership with respect to management participation and the matter of control.

3. Taxation. Taxes must always be considered. For example, if the decision is made to acquire a firm through assets, the buyer may be required to pay general sales tax (a GST is common in most industrialized countries), whereas when purchasing through acquired shares, generally GST is not applicable. The method used for the acquisition and time (relative to the tax year) of the purchase must be considered as well.

4. Share structure for the new company. For a new company, it is better to have a high equity-debt ratio, because it gives a better financial status. At the same time, the new owner/manager should negotiate a line of credit sufficient to give the company a comfortable position. Once obtained, the available funds may not

be required to meet the ongoing need. It is also better to negotiate with the bank (or any financial institution) when the firm is in a comfortable position rather than in a state of "desperation".

5. Company's organization. Capital structure affects the firm's organization. In particular, this is true if the investors wish to participate in management. An effective organization is always an organization that facilitates communication and provides a healthy working environment. A simple structure is always better than an overly elaborate reporting system, particularly for small firms. In other words, from the point of view of the organization structure, it should be designed to be manageable with respect to present available human capacity.

6. Reason for selling the business. Health reasons, lack of interest, succession problems, lack of profit, or because the product reached the end of its product life cycle; these are all possible reasons for selling the business. Knowing the reason for selling the business will give a better guide to evaluating the potential of the firm under consideration.

7. Prepare a check list to ensure all considerations are being covered under the circumstances. This is only a short list of things to be done when considering the acquisition of an existing business. When purchasing a used car, the seller must include a mechanical fitness certificate. Since no fitness certificate can be obtained when acquiring a business, the buyer of the business should exercise some discipline to make it a happy marriage.

To be a franchisee is an easier way to enter into a business, though being a franchisee is considered to be the same as buying yourself a job without the union rights. Nevertheless, franchising is here to stay. Research has proven that a franchise business experiences a lower failure rate than other small businesses. At any rate, to purchase a franchising right requires a substantial initial investment (franchising fee). Whilst a large financial investment is a commitment in itself, the franchisee would have to have more concern for the operation, since purchasing the franchising right may wipe out his entire savings or maybe worse. Moreover, since riding on a successful person's coat-tails always has trade-offs, it is always better to start up a new business. Under the circumstances, before entering into an agreement with the franchisor, the would-be franchisee should consider the following:

1. The franchisor's success record. Of course, the more successful it is, the higher the fees that would have to be paid.

2. Territory protection. Be fully aware of territory protection in order to prevent the franchisor from selling another agreement to someone else just next door to your outlet when you have nearly killed yourself working hard to make it a success.
3. The franchisor's side of the agreement. Make sure that it is honoured.
4. Legal advice. Engage a competent lawyer who knows about franchising to go over the agreement before signing it.

Being a franchisor is quite different from being a franchisee. A franchisee can be a simple franchisee (as a job) or a master franchisee. A master franchisee is one who holds several franchised agreements (operating several outlets) under one franchisor.

When a franchisor franchises a product or service this is essentially a marketing method; it expands a business by using someone else's money. It cannot be disputed that franchising has a strong hold in the marketplace. If in any event an individual wishes to establish a successful franchising operation, he should first have an established operation, a well-structured, reasonable and attractive franchising package, a good reputable promoter and, above all, develop a good, honest record on servicing the franchisees. In some countries, government agencies are available to assist would-be franchisors design a franchising package and other services. Otherwise, if one does not wish to do it alone, professional help is always available for a fee.

Ongoing Management

Ventures start up small and are managed by the owner/entrepreneur. But as the firm grows to a size beyond the owner/manager's mental and physical capacity, the expansion is often an even greater challenge than starting up. As someone said: "It is easy to get there, but can you hang on?" To better manage a growing firm without losing its entrepreneurial drive is a real challenge. This aspect has been discussed in chapter 9. The delegation and control of an entrepreneur-managed firm will be dealt with in this chapter.

Delegation

Do we know how to delegate? The answer is yes and no. Yes, because we all know how to tell people to do this or that. No, because once we tell people to do this or that, we tend to nag like a stereotypical mother-in-law or a back-seat driver. Proper delegation in an entrepreneur-managed firm must include the following steps to make the delegation effective:

Stage one
- Find a key individual in the firm in whom the entrepreneur has full confidence.
- If necessary, retain a professional person.
- The key individual works with the professional person (if any) to create the reorganization plan.

Stage two
- Discuss with the key person, delegating reorganization responsibility.
- Involve middle managers, explain why reorganization is necessary (the CEO with the key person's presence).
- Middle managers and supervisory staff write their own job descriptions, including personal objectives, and how they see themselves in the new organizational structure.
- Meet with middle managers and supervisors, and work with key individuals to map out a reorganizational plan.

Stage three
- Delegate decision making.
- Implement reorganization plan and specify reporting system.
- Install control systems:
  - Responsibility centres
  - Formalized reporting system
  - Feedback system
  - Back-up system
- Break organization into smaller units.
- Encourage entrepreneurial initiatives.
- Practise positive reinforcement.

The Matter of Professional Management

People tend to criticise most small entrepreneur-managed firms for being unable or unwilling to practise professional management. While professional management provides a great deal of incentive to the entrepreneur/manager, it may escape notice that this dehumanizes the firm as the firm grows to the size where it isolates people from the organization, and worse still, isolates people from people. Table 10.2 provides a list of strengths and weaknesses of professionalization.

Table 10.2
Strengths and weaknesses of professionalization.

Strengths	Weaknesses
Less human error, more systematic approach to management	Dehumanizes the organization and erodes the individual's ability to make discretionary decisions
Helps the firm be better organized	Rarely challenges the establishment
Helps implement ideas	Seldom stimulates ideas
Improves operational results, if used to guide actions	Presupposes conformity to accepted standards
Helps to organize thoughts and better manages time and effort, thus improving resource allocation	In extreme instances, discourages creativity
Helps to make risk more manageable	Shuns risk
Improves the chances of success, which in itself is an element of motivation	Cannot measure individual motivation and is intolerant of deviation
More disciplined approach to the pursuit of opportunity	Misses opportunities

Source: Modified from Kao (1989: 11).

The Transition from Hands-on to Professional Management

With knowledge of the strengths and weaknesses of the professional approach to business management, the following are a few simple notes that entrepreneur/managers should observe when the transition takes place from a hands-on management style to a more professionally oriented management practice. The purpose is to make it possible for entrepreneurial drive to flourish in the firm, while the professionalized management approach is under consideration.

- The entrepreneur/manager should be aware that it is the "people" who are in transition, not the firm.
- All individuals in the firm must be involved in the transition process.
- An individual must be able to identify with the transition.
- An individual must be able to identify with the firm.

○ An individual must be able to identify with the entrepreneur/ manager.

○ The owner/manager must be able to identify with any individual in the firm.

○ An entrepreneurial firm is a human institution and, therefore, no attempt should be made to dehumanize the firm.

○ An attempt must be made to enhance an individual's entrepreneurial attributes as discussed in Chapter 9.

○ The development of the individual's entrepreneurial skills through work assignment or other forms of involvement must continue.

○ Opportunities for the firm as well as for the individual must still be pursued.

The bottom line is, by all means consider professional management practices, but never make any individual a "professional person" or a "professional manager". A person is a human being, and humanity must be part of being human.

Will the Jobs Ever Come Back?

A prominent headline in *Time* magazine in February 1994 read: "Will jobs ever come back?" To people who ask this question, the answer is "Yes" and "No". Some of those on the unemployment line may have an opportunity once the economy turns around, but for others, the job loss could be permanent, either because of the nature of the job, the age of the person, or other circumstances. The shocking part lies in two other headlines: "Governments want to retain jobs; industry wants to lose jobs" and "Our future is in a more educated work force". In Canada, due to US subsidiaries moving south of the border (the US and Mexico), even top executives are jobless and, consequently, there has been a large number of management consultants emerging in major Canadian centres. The article goes to give a jobs lost count around the world, including Daimler-Benz's plans to eliminate 50,000 jobs on top of the 20,000 it has so far targeted. The German metal industry is cutting 600,000, and an additional half a million workers will be put on "short time". The payroll at Fiat, Italy's largest private employer, has declined since 1989 from 117,000 to 95,000. Last October the French government tried to trim 4,000 jobs from overstaffed Air France. The job situation is not a problem unique to North America, though with the free trade move between Canada and the US and the signing of NAFTA, who knows how many jobs will disappear and whether those jobs will ever come back? What does this mean to people? To some of them, job loss is a permanent status unless, of course, they prepare to do something for themselves instead of relying on large firms or governments to create jobs for them. The fact is that "jobs lost in large corporations are not exceptions but rather the rule", because decision makers, if not always, usually put profit before people. Can you blame them? A capitalist society is capital driven. Why should capitalists put people before profit? Incidentally, in January 1994, the Finance Minister of Canada called together a group of business people and economists to an open forum discussion about Canada's economy and jobs. A bank president said to the Minister: "Invest in education, we need better educated people for more demanding jobs." The Minister responded: "My son is a university graduate with an engineering degree, and he too doesn't have a job."

The wonderful thing of being a human and being in a democratic society is that we could always make some (if not all) decisions for ourselves, and having one's own business is a case in point. With careful planning and management, and by looking for an available market niche such as developing an environmentally friendly product, providing environmentally friendly service, or computer support systems, having your own business will not give you the highway to heaven, but it is surely a vehicle to economic freedom. A look at the people of Taiwan, Thailand and the rest of the Pacific Rim should be sufficient encouragement for job hunters and others to give the creation of your own venture a try. However, one may ask, if I decide to go into a business on my own, will I be as successful as Morita (the person who with his partner Ibuka brought Sony from its obscure beginning in 1946 to international prominence by the late 1960s), or Henry Ford? The answer is no because there is only one Morita and only one Henry Ford. Then, one may ask: Can I be assured that I will be successful in my endeavour? The answer is yes and no. Yes, you can be successful but first you must establish your own success criteria. No, there is no assurance you will be successful, because success is mainly dependent on your own efforts. Then why should anyone bother with all this if there is no guarantee of success? The answer is simple — in the lottery, if you do not have a ticket, you cannot win. This is true in business as well . But while in the lottery, once you buy the ticket you are in the hands of God, in business you and God work together as partners.

Appendix

Questions Need Expression of Your Thoughts, but Not Necessarily Absolute Answers

Preamble

Life is a journey on earth. We all hold a one-way ticket with no fixed date for "journey's end". Unfortunately, in reality, not only is there no one who can sell us a return ticket, but we are also not given the right to make our own "journey's end" decision (to commit suicide; a person can be punished by law in some countries after an unsuccessful suicide attempt). The journey begins with our parents' blessings and the duration differs from one person to another. For some, the journey may last only one day (or even less than a day), others may be on the road for as long as one hundred years or more. We hear a lot about others' "journey's ends", but never our own.

During this life journey on earth, I am quite sure every one of us has a lot of questions, such as: Why are we here on earth? Is there any real purpose in life? What is happiness? Why do some people have so much and others have none? What is profit? Why is entrepreneurship so important to our economy? Why should we make so much fuss about entrepreneurial attributes when, after all, every single individual has more or less such attributes? Should we always put money before people? Why do business people in Japan continue their desire for more, even though they have already drained 16 per cent of the world's total materials? In 1992, the Japanese manufacturers used only 10 per cent of their 711 million tons of imported raw materials as export products, and may have wasted 90 per cent of raw materials which could have been used for other purposes (see also Hitomi, 1994: 5).

Some questions will eventually find answers that work well. For example, why should we always talk about equality, when we know perfectly well equality occurs only at birth and death and inequality begins the minute we are born and ends the day we die? Nevertheless, inequality creates opportunities. There will always be countless individuals with no financial means to go through formal education, but because of their determination, hard work, imagination, and commitment, they are able to succeed in their endeavours. In fact, more often than not, it is the dissatisfaction with inequality experienced in life that generates creativity and initiates change. On the other hand, there are also countless unanswered questions because answers are hard to find or cannot be found.

There is one issue that has puzzled me for at least several decades. This issue, derived from Tolstoy's (the author of *War and Peace*) work, is: "I hate to be a physician; when I cure the poor, they will be exploited by the rich, and if I cure the rich, they will continue to exploit the poor." How can we resolve this dilemma? However, there is a simple answer to this: A physician's oath is to cure the sick and save lives regardless of the patient's status. Then, what about Tolstoy's concern? Is it true or false?

Another interesting thing in life is our concern with profit. Though we admit that J. R. Hicks is right about his definition of profit, the truth is that no one in this life will make any profit — we came with nothing and will go with nothing. Since we are all not "as well off at the end as we were at the beginning", where is the profit? Perhaps the meaningful thing in this life is not how much profit we should make, but what can we do to make life more meaningful for ourselves as well as for others. I cannot imagine that a person who is ranked by others to be worth US$50 billion in assets still wants greater wealth. The question is if such wealth does not come from other people, it must come from the environment. How long can this go on? Can anyone honestly say: I want all the happiness in the world (money and ...) and let the rest of the world go begging on their knees (including the environment)?

The appended are a series of questions prepared for us to examine ourselves as agents of creation in the interest of the individual and adding value to society. Some of the questions are controversial, but none seeks perfect answers. In fact, there are no perfect answers, but by exposing ourselves to these challenges and discussing them, we may have better answers.

Chapter 1

1. What is fair representation? Can democracy be exercised under the condition of fair representation?

2. Explain the term "majority rule" and how it works in organizations such as:

   ○ Stockholding companies
   ○ Entrepreneur-managed firms
   ○ Organizations created not for profit
   ○ Government and government agencies
   ○ Countries such as the US, Korea and your own country

3. How can a political system influence the market economy, develop, cultivate and nurture entrepreneurship?

4. Cuba is still a country ruled by the Communist Party. Assume that you are engaged as a consultant to work on a master plan to develop entrepreneurship in Cuba. What model will you use to accomplish your task? Discuss.

5. Can we put political freedom before economic freedom? Is it possible for a democratic government, claimed by so many political leaders to help its people, to acquire economic freedom since the people can be free to choose who should govern them?

6. Does the market economy give people the economic freedom they need? Discuss.

7. What is the role of a government, be it democratic or communist, in developing entrepreneurship? Compare the differences in government policy for developing entrepreneurship between any countries you know. Should there be any difference(s)?

8. Under the democratic framework as you know it, is it correct to say that we are living under a capital-driven economy? Therefore, democracy used in the political system cannot be exercised in the board room. The truth of the matter is: although we fought so hard and lost millions or more lives to gain an inch for the right to elect

people to govern us, we have lost our freedom to decide on our economic future. Do you agree? Why?

9. Some people say that Russia has tried hard to model itself on "western democracy" but unfortunately, it has lost the ability to make economic decisions for its people. On the other hand, not wishing to copy "western democracy", China's leader makes economic decisions for its people. Do you agree? Explain why investors from all over the world, many "bred and raised in western democracy", prefer to invest in China rather than in Russia.

10. Entrepreneurship is a matter of mindset and it is a natural ability possessed by every individual by virtue of birth. Do you agree? Why?

   Perhaps you should do research on this and report it at an international conference. The title could be: Economic development of China and democratic countries around the world in the twenty-first century. Who knows, you may be a candidate for the Nobel prize in economics or political science.

Chapter 2

1. Since energy is creative in nature, therefore we are naturally creative. Use your personal experiences to answer the following questions:

   (a) How creative am I? How do my creations benefit myself (need not be financially) and add value to society (society can be interpreted as group, school, organization, community, your own country and the world).

   (b) What are the incidents that have hindered, damaged or killed your initiative and creative desire?

   (c) With reference to (b) above, what did you do to overcome these hindrances, obstacles and/or forces that damaged or killed your initiative?

   (d) In the event that you are now not as creative as you used to be because of various reasons you found in (b) above, if those incidents had not happened, what would you have done with your excess energy?

2. John F. Bulloch, President of the Canadian Federation of Independent Business, an entrepreneur in his own right, once defined entrepreneurship as being:

   Total scar tissue divided by total body area = 1

What does it mean? How does it apply to your own experience?

3. Both standardization and professionalized practice of human endeavours arise from need. The strongest argument to support standardization and professionalism has been and always will be: to protect public interest and serve consumers. Discuss. If you agree with the argument, what should a professional organization do to permit entrepreneurial drive to flourish within the profession?

4. The "entity" concept is an accounting postulate, as well as a status for an incorporated business in the course of law, but it was economics, through the theory of the firm, that gave the blessing to both. Since then, a corporation is an entity, much the same as a person functioning in the marketplace, but it is a human that pulls the string. Under the circumstances, a serious question is raised: What is the responsibility of a corporation if its activity causes harm to the environment? The answer is: It can be punished by law once convicted, including fine, jail sentence (licence suspension) and/or death sentence (revoke its licence or charter). But since it is not the same as a person, because it has no feelings, passion, love or any human assets, what should we do? Should we abolish the "entity" concept and treat every corporation as an extension of human beings? Discuss.

5. What is the impact of the theory of the firm on business management? Does the theory of the firm have anything to do with entrepreneurship? Discuss.

6. What is profit? Should it only be the entitlement to the shareholders' investment? Discuss.

7. Were the entrepreneurs who created businesses stimulated by the lure of profits? Discuss.

8. In the socialist state, it is the state which takes the harvest whereas under the theory of the firm, it is the firm or, more specifically, the equity holders who are entitled to the residual of a firm's operation. Therefore, the theory of the firm, maybe not by design, pushes the power source of human institutions into a triangle forging themselves through the firm (represented by people selected by shareholders), the union and the government. In your opinion, is this the ideal direction that human institutions should develop and continue? There is also a fundamental question that should be addressed: Should workers work for a living or bargain with the firm's management for a living? Discuss.

9. If you are a corporate executive, what is your major concern: compete

for money in the capital market, commit yourself to the continuing pursuit of opportunity and/or develop an enterprise so both you and the enterprise can be proud of each other? (The answer should not be: "If I have money, everything else will come naturally.")

10. How do investors invest? Assume two corporations are competing for funds in the marketplace. One corporation stresses earning annual profit and paying dividends to its shareholders at an above average rate, while the other corporation is more interested in investing in the future, such as: employees' development, allocating a share of profit for protection of the environment, but not too much emphasis is placed on short term profit or dividends. Which of these two corporations attracts more investors? (The question is recognized as being overly simplified but it is worth the discussion.)

Chapter 3

1. What is the roundabout process in the theory of capital? Why is this so important in determining corporate profit? How meaningful is it to managers of the firm, learners and academics? Discuss.

2. Why has the accounting profession as a whole not made up its mind about the recognition of "opportunity cost" as an eligible sacrifice for doing business? Discuss.

3. Those businesses with detrimental effect on the environment, for example, loggers, manufacturers of chemical products, petroleum and its by-products, and the auto industry, all have an impressive plea for their concern for employment. In some cases, the dispute between an industry and the environmental protectionists can go as far as appealing to our judicial system for help. In your opinion, how far can we rely on the judicial system to protect our environment? Assume an expert witness in a court case describing passionately the importance of employment as follows: "We realize there is a promised land, but if we are dead, how can we get there? Without employment, there will be no food on the table. What shall we do? To address the future alone without concern to the present is simply naive at its best." Discuss.

4. In the interest of our environment and the life support for our future, environmentalists have done their part to stimulate the general awareness of the concerned. The real fundamental challenge still rests on how we perceive profit. Under the circumstances, we cannot take accounting profit (income) seriously, because the accounting practice has no consideration for environmental costs before

deriving a corporate profit. There is not much hope from the economists because model builders are still very much interested in GNP or GDP without factoring environmental loss into their calculation. What can be done to convince both the accountants and the economists to have mercy on the environment before "profit"?

5. What is the role of our "B" schools, the cradle of our future business executives, in respect of profit determination? How should they design their curriculum in order to reflect their concern for our future?

6. Investors are interested in nothing but profit. What kind of profit are they interested in? Should investors be concerned about our environment?

7. Real estate speculators are more often than not able to realize large sums of profit. Does this form of profit add any value to society? Discuss.

8. In theory, no one can possibly determine profit adequately since, in essence, we are unable to adequately aggregate residuals of production factors. One person might say: Who cares? Others may react differently, saying: We do. We know perfectly well no one can live forever. The ancient monarchs wanted to but failed. Today we do the same. The medical profession would agree with you; they will do anything they can to save lives. Beauticians will do anything they can to make people stay young and beautiful forever which is, in effect, human efforts against nature. The point is, just because we know it cannot be done should not prevent us from trying. Then, what have accountants and economists done with respect to the true meaning of profit to humanity? Knowing perfectly well, if our environment is deteriorating, and life support is eroding at a rapid rate, why are they still waving the big flag for profit to the firm, and ROI to its shareholders, while the firm's product selling in the market either came from the depletion of our natural assets, or ripping off the environment? And have the economists made any attempt to reveal that by eroding our life support, there will be no profit at all? Discuss.

9. What is visional profit? How does one build an entrepreneurial vision into a profit model so the entrepreneur can justify his entitlement of the profit? Discuss.

10. Define morality and profit in your own terms, then discuss their relationship and how they shape one's decision making behaviour in business.

Chapter 4

1. At a board meeting of a large corporation whose rate of return on investment happened to be below expectation, the board members were quite upset about the firm's performance and questioned the CEO: Why could we not meet shareholders' expectation? Is it possible for us to maintain our share value in the marketplace? The CEO, on the advice of the corporate controller, responded to the board: "Our controller has already engaged an outside consultant to do a thorough analysis and will advise me of the proper cause of action based on the analysis. In fact, I intend to make a report at our next board meeting." The board accepted the CEO's reply and the meeting was adjourned.

    The board met again one month later. The CEO made a brief report by saying: During the past years we have spent a great deal of money engaging in R&D activities, and we expect to generate significant revenue in the next three to five years. A large amount of R&D spending was expended in their respective years and the same treatment was applied to advertising expenses. In accordance with our fiscal spending estimates, the forthcoming year should also see substantial R&D and advertising expenditures, but after discussions with our marketing V-P, we feel that we are now at the end of the tunnel, so I have decided to halt any additional R&D expenditure, and also cap the amount of advertising expenditure. Furthermore, according to the consultant, certain R&D items should not have been expended but should have been deferred. Adjustments have been made by the controller's office and you will see that we shall be able to give our shareholders the ROI that they expect.

    Discuss the CEO's response to the board, the consultant's report and his action with respect to the improvement of the ROI.

2. Assume you have created a viable business for yourself, followed a golden rule and are very cautious about the way your venture is financed. Your priorities are: cash first, profit second, rate of return on capital investment last. One day, a venture capitalist offered you $5 million for 30 per cent of equity, but with a number of restrictive covenants. The good thing was that with additional funds, you could improve the rate of return on investment substantially, but you turned the offer down. When you told a friend about the incident, he could not understand why you were not interested in a high rate of return on your investment. Try to explain to your friend why you refused the offer.

3. A stock exchange is merely a marketplace where buyers and sellers

meet. It is governed by the stock exchange commission (or some other organization with a different name but having the same function). One such function is to regulate corporate reporting. Should the stock exchange take action to require a full disclosure of a firm's commitment to the protection of the environment? Discuss.

4. What is the relationship between the theory of the firm and the theories of management?

5. What is a general management model? If the model is being developed based on the general management framework, then why is this framework necessary?

6. Why is there so much advancement in technology and science and so little work done in skills and practices in business management? Discuss.

7. Is ROI a demon to humanity? Discuss.

8. If you are a member of the accounting standards committee of an international accounting body, what would you do to improve ROI through reshaping the accounting theory? What would be your recommendations?

9. Assuming you are an economist with a flair for accounting, and a man compared your brainchild ROI with war. He said: "Today, it seems fashionable to compare military strategy with strategies used in business, but there is a difference. War strategies are designed to win but people are killed, whilst business strategies are also designed to win, the end result being a lot of profit. Superficially business strategies do not do what war does — kill people. Unfortunately, excessive demand for profit and ROI kills the environment and life support. When the environment and life support are gone, we will all die unless business strategists could make businesses earn profit on one hand and be good to the environment on the other." What do you think of his comment? What should you do with this man?

10. If you are the manager of a division of a multinational corporation and you are unable to improve sales or reduce current cost, what would you do?

Chapter 5

1. Why is a proper definition of an "entrepreneur" important?

2. What is moderated risk? Examine it from all aspects when undertaking any endeavour. Make whatever assumptions you deem necessary.

3. There has been some concern about people who do not possess the right attributes to start up their business, and who consequently fail in their first attempt. On the other hand, many people do have the right attributes but also fail in their business ventures. What do you consider to be the right attributes? Discuss the importance of having the right attributes.

4. Examine Table 5.1. Assume the summary is well represented. Define an entrepreneur and explain your definition. If you do not favour any of the definitions including the one given by the author, please explain why.

5. Please refer to Table 5.3. Once the author made a presentation at a seminar designed exclusively for entrepreneurship researchers. Upon completion of the presentation, an internationally renowned professor asked the author: "What do these researchers do under the circumstances?" Assume you are one of the researchers in the seminar, what should you do? One of the answers could be: "Don't do any more research, get on with it and start up your own business."

6. Please refer to Figures 5.1 and 5.2. Assume you are the CEO of an organization experiencing the same organizational overload and "incommunicable interdepartmental communication". What should you do to improve this line of telephone communication and what should you do with your organization? Discuss.

7. Compare a profit centre with a corporate unit (or a corporation) which preaches the practice of intrepreneurship. Then ask yourself a fundamental question: Would the head office be willing to give up the idea of using the internal rate of return on investment to measure the performance of a unit manager of a corporation? If your answer is "yes", what should it use instead? If your answer is "no", explain whether the head office should stay with the idea, let the unit be a profit centre and forget about intrepreneurship.

8. Comment on the author's definition of entrepreneurship and the entrepreneur. Support your comments with your reasons (you may wish to read Appendix 5.1 to this chapter first).

9. "An entrepreneur is a troublemaker." Discuss.

10. If you feel you are a trouble maker, but you are creative and whatever you create adds value to society, then are you a true entrepreneur?

Otherwise, cause more troubles, but be sure it creates wealth for yourself and adds value to the world.

Chapter 6

1. Study the fisherman's conversation with the author. What motivates him to do what he does?

2. An individual who is not an authority on human behaviour suggested the following: "Every individual can be motivated, but first we have to know the individual's needs. The trouble is, we do not always know what a person's real needs are. If things get serious enough, questions about the individual's needs become more challenging: Firstly, we do not know the difference between needs and wants. Economists would say this question is easy to answer, then you may wish to forget it. Secondly, even if you are told what his needs are, you do not know whether he is telling a lie or not telling the truth. Then you may not know the difference between an outright lie and not telling the truth. Thirdly, even if you know his needs, what can you do to motivate the individual to be creative or, more specifically, to create a business and run it?"

   Make any assumption in order for you to give a meaningful response.

3. Can our legal system provide people with positive motivation? For example, instead of fearing punishment, people may be eager to do things of value that earn rewards. Rewards do not necessarily mean money, knighthood, or canonization after death.

4. "Justice Bao", a soap opera that has run for over 200 episodes, is the most watched television programme in Taiwan. What motivates people to watch that programme? If you are not acquainted with the programme, the general idea is that Justice Bao represents justice.

5. A tourism expert told a group of hotel operators what to expect when dealing with Japanese tourists: "Don't be surprised if they ask to be lodged in Japanese hotels. This seldom applies to tourists from other countries. There are tourists concerned about room rates, four- or five-star hotels or other forms of conveniences, such as shopping." Why is there a difference in behaviour?

6. In one primary research conducted to investigate university business students' career choice upon graduation, none of the 160 first-year undergraduate sample group expressed their willingness to start

their own businesses. On the other hand, better results were obtained from college and secondary school students in the area of creating new ventures. Why? One professor from a well-known university told his audience frankly: "Our curriculum is designed primarily to turn out graduates to run other people's business." Comment.

7. Please read Appendix 5.2 to Chapter 5 and comment from your own point of view. The bottom-line questions are:

   (a) Do we need to reassess our business schools' commitment to business education? Are basic changes required to improve their service to society and to the world?

   (b) If your answer to (a) is yes, what should we do to introduce the changes?

   (c) What changes are needed to replace the current practice?

8. What motivates people in Southeast Asian countries to commit themselves to the economic good of the individual and the country, or even of the region as a whole? Give reasons to support your answer.

9. Canada has an excellent welfare programme, in particular its unemployment insurance scheme, but some people take advantage of the system. They work during the summer and make sure they are unemployed in winter so as to collect unemployment insurance benefits and go to Florida to enjoy the sun and heat. The government has tried all it could to correct the situation but it is still difficult to prevent abuse. Therefore, concerned individuals are wondering whether it is all that good for the government to look after its needy citizens. Comment.

10. Try to do a simple study between males and females with respect to their interest in creating new businesses. Examine their reasons for wanting to start up a business using the same criteria as illustrated in Table 6.2.

Chapter 7

1. Ownership is one of the visible and important factors of motivation. It is an established fact that everyone strives for ownership: Home, car, personal property, reputation and title are just a few examples. Why is it so important to own something? Discuss.

2. Geographers believe that as human beings we have the choice of either changing ourselves to fit into the environment, or changing the environment to suit our needs. Discuss.

3. Examine Figure 7.3. What is the role of an entrepreneur (from the point of view of creating wealth for the individual and adding value to society) in matters of conservation, innovation and creations which stretch the life support supply line?

4. Discuss the various forms of ownership acquisition and owners' responsibility toward what they own. (All acquisitions must be legal as well as meaningful to the individual, society and the environment.)

5. Develop a series of environmentally friendly products or services with the purpose of promoting environmental health, and the possibility of developing them into viable business ventures.

6. Discuss the similarities and differences between owning a job and owning a business.

7. In a sense, through conceptual arguments, mathematical manipulation and the support of professional bodies, through satisfying consumers' needs and wants and generating profit for investors, we have in effect dehumanized institutions. Is it possible to put humanity back into the dehumanized institutions? If not, what will happen if the trend continues?

8. Do you agree that the real meaning of life is sharing? What are the advantages and disadvantages of sharing business ownership?

9. Ownership means decision making. With ownership, we can make decisions for what we own. Do you agree? Why?

10. If earth is our home, why does every country have immigration rules? Discuss.

Chapter 8

1. What is a discretionary decision? In business, who should make discretionary decisions?

2. If the higher authority in an institution did not delegate discretionary decision making to his or her subordinates, what would happen, if the subordinates refuse to make any discretionary decision? Discuss.

3. In one entrepreneur-managed firm, the owner/entrepreneur bitterly complained that he had not been able to take a holiday for at least ten years. In his words: "I am like a parent with a whole bunch of babies, they just cannot do anything without me." What is wrong with this firm? What is wrong with the firm's management?

4. Comment on the following statement: "An entrepreneurial decision is making a decision for the good of others; personal risk is more often than not, not part of the decision."

5. In marketing, when a product manager decides to launch a new product, what does he have in mind, the consumer's interest or the interest of the shareholders? Discuss.

6. Discuss the criteria for success. What is personal success, society's success, a nation's success and the success of humanity as a whole?

7. In a government committee meeting to select the recipient of an entrepreneurship award, the criteria were: owning a business, risk-taking, financial success (profit, ROI, etc.) and a few other requirements. Among the committee members, financial success was considered an important factor. One member seriously supported entrepreneur A whose financial performance was mediocre but he managed to venture into the unknown. For example, he launched a large number of environmentally friendly products into new markets and new territories. Other members supported entrepreneur B, a retailer enjoying very healthy sales with a very impressive profit performance but serving an existing market. Who do you support? Why?

8. Can entrepreneurial attributes be developed? What is the purpose of developing entrepreneurial attributes? What is the role of parents, educational institutions and society in developing entrepreneurial attributes?

9. Based on your personal experience, do you agree that the fear of risk is always greater than the risk itself? Discuss.

10. Entrepreneurs are fast learners but they do not pay attention to matters of no relevance to them. Why? What other entrepreneurial attributes may be used to help you explain the above?

Chapter 9

1. Why should creativity be associated with passion?

2. Based on the author's teaching, business and consulting experiences, he concluded that almost without exception, all entrepreneurs are passionately in love with their own businesses, to the extent of working long hours, including working in their dreams. Even though at times, the businesses gave them a lot of trouble and affected their health, took away their leisure time, family life and required many

other personal sacrifices, they carried on with the business without complaining. Discuss why passion and love are not included as entrepreneurial attributes.

3. Assume you are a corporate decision maker in a controlling position, even though you are not the majority shareholder. Do you favour the idea of sharing the harvest with all those working in the firm? Why? If you agree with the idea of sharing the harvest, please describe how you would go about it.

4. Assume you have a good understanding about accounting practice. Do you feel that the stakeholders' interest should be represented in the company's statement of position (balance sheet)? If so, how should it be represented?

5. There is universal behavioural expectation associated with our need for survival. The ownership desire, however, varies among individuals. There are people who want to own the world, others may just simply wish to own the bare essentials, such as toothbrush, eyeglasses and simple clothing. These are, nevertheless, desires for ownership. Is ownership an absolute or a relative? Explain.

6. In the UK, there was a period when a significant number of large corporations had divisions with performances which were far below expectation. Under the circumstances, a few companies decided to close down some unprofitable divisions. A few others were willing to salvage the situation by discussing with division managers about putting up some funds from their own pockets and taking the division out of the company, creating a new, smaller company or a spin-off. According to the report given by a banker at a small academic gathering in Europe, the spin-off companies were doing quite well. Why has the practice not gained popularity in the UK or other parts of the world? Contribute what you know about this practice.

7. How do we develop entrepreneurial attributes among the working population in large corporations and/or other organizations? Who should benefit from it? Discuss.

8. Is it possible to develop an individual's "risk-taking" attribute? If so, what can be done to increase an individual's willingness to take risks? There are always some people who may say: "I have been burnt once, not a second time, please!" Discuss.

9. How important is it to develop the required entrepreneurial skills through formal education? Suggest ways to help yourself and others improve entrepreneurial skills such as interpersonal and communication skills through informal learning.

10. In accordance with your perception, describe the UN's role in connection with environmental and planetary rights. What should the UN do if multinational corporations seriously damage our life support and the national government which has jurisdiction over the matter fails to take action? Discuss.

Chapter 10

1. It is believed that people who start up a business do not normally go through a formal approach such as: developing a product concept, testing it, doing a feasibility study, then a business plan, etc. Moreover, researchers tend to suggest that there is a high failure rate for new businesses within the first three years of operation. Do you feel there is any proven relationship between ill-prepared business start-ups and small-business failures?

2. Some people say that to have a successful start-up of a new venture, all you need are people and money, that is, determined venture founders and adequate start-up financing. Do you agree? Discuss.

3. What is a business plan? In one of the author's books, he suggested that a business plan must be prepared with the user's needs in mind. But after some firsthand experience, it was noted that more often than not, money suppliers (such as bankers) were interested in a business plan merely for supplementary information. In fact, a good collateral is all it needs to get bank financing. Do you agree? Why? Why is a business plan important?

4. If you have the money, how would you start up a business?

5. A good government with excellent government officials is necessary to provide the right environment to encourage individuals to take risks and start their own businesses. Do you agree?

6. With reference to question 5, an autocratic government with a sense of direction can lead the country to better economic development, in particular, to stimulate entrepreneurial drive. Dissatisfaction with autocratic leadership and complaints create opportunities for change. Discuss.

7. The leaders of democratic countries tend to believe that it is democracy that creates the investment climate that stimulates profitable opportunities thus creating a favourable business environment. Discuss.

8. Dream up a business and create a business plan (a) for your own personal use and (b) to attract investors. While preparing the plan, you should consider the following points:

- Speak your mind.
- Show your determination, commitment, and competence.
- Show your passion and love for what you plan to do.
- A plan must have a set of cash flow projections (if you do not know, you can always try to give an educated guess, for three years on a month by month basis if possible).
- A plan should have a clear flow of ideas and good co-ordination.
- It should be written so that it is clear, complete, and correct (if that is not possible, guess, but state the basis for the guesswork).
- Follow up with an action plan (when to do what).

9. Develop a simple financing scheme for your would-be viable enterprise. It can be as simple as:

Funds required for		Sources of funds	
Building a prototype	$ 10,000	Personal savings	$ 5,000
Registration	1,000	Love money (from parents)	20,000
Market test	1,000	Partner's contribution	10,000
Feasibility study	2,000	Selling of personal assets	20,000
Rent in advance	3,000	Bank loan	30,000
Stationery	1,000		
Promotion expenses	5,000		
First-year operation	60,000		
Contingencies	2,000		
Total	$ 85,000	Total	$85,000

10. Assume your would-be business is a high technology project that will be good for the environment. It is electronic, not chemical, and you wish to take this product into the world market. What should you do to make your dream a reality?

References

Alderfer, Clayton P. (1972), *Existence, Relatedness and Growth, Human Needs in Organizational Setting*, New York: Free Press.

Baumol (1968), "Entrepreneurship and Economic Theory", *American Economic Review*, Vol. 58, pp. 64–71.

Bowles, Samuel and Herbert Gintis (1986), *Democracy and Capitalism*, New York: Basic Books.

Cantillon, R. (1931), *Essai sur la Nature du Commerce en General*, tran. Henry Higgs, London: Macmillan, first published 1755.

Chan, Kwok Bun and Claire Chiang (1994), *Stepping Out: The Making of Chinese Entrepreneurs*, Singapore: Prentice Hall.

Clifton, Carr and Tom Turner (1990), *Wild by Law*, San Francisco: Sierra Club Books.

Dahl, Robert A. (1915), *Democracy and its Critics*, New Haven: Yale University Press.

Gibb, A.A. (1986/87), "Education for Enterprise: Training for Small Business

Initiation — Some Contrasts", *Journal of Small Business and Entrepreneurship*, Vol. 4, No. 3, pp. 42–8.

Gibb, A.A. (1990), "Entrepreneurship and Intrepreneurship — Exploring the Differences", in *New Findings and Perspectives in Entrepreneurship*, edited by Rik Donckels and A. Miettinen, Aldershot: Avebury.

Gray, Charlotte (1993), "Living for Todai", *Saturday Night*, Toronto, June.

Hepp, Gerald W. and Thomas W. McRae (1982), "Accounting Standards Overload: Relief Needed", *Journal of Accountancy*, May, p. 62.

Hicks, J.R. (1950), *Value and Capital*, 2nd Edition, Oxford: Oxford University Press.

Hitomi, K. (1994), "Japan's Manufacturers Should Be Doing More with Less", *Business Week*, 10 January, p. 5.

Kao, Raymond W.Y. (1980), *Accounting Standards Overload*, Vancouver: Accounting Standards Authority of Canada.

Kao, Raymond W.Y. (1984), *Small Business Management: A Strategic Emphasis*, 2nd Edition, Toronto: Holt, Rinehart and Winston.

Kao, Raymond W.Y. (1986), "Strategic Issues in Financial Management for Starting and Managing New Small Ventures", *Canadian Treasury Management Review*, Royal Bank of Canada, November, Special Edition, pp. 1–4.

Kao, Raymond W.Y. (1989), *Entrepreneurship and Enterprise Development*, Toronto: Holt, Rinehart and Winston.

Kao, Raymond W.Y. (1993), "Defining Entrepreneurship: Past, Present and ?", *Creativity and Innovation Management*, 2(1).

Kay Shuyin, Lim Siang Peng, Glen and Alice Tay, supervised by Wong Soke-yin (1994), *The Singapore Entrepreneur: Skills, Attitudes and Behaviours*, Singapore: School of Accountancy and Business, Nanyang Technological University, unpublished.

Kierstead, B.S. (1959), *Capital, Interest and Profits*, Oxford: Blackwell.

Kirzner, Israel (1973), *Competition and Entrepreneurship*, Chicago: University of Chicago Press.

Kirzner, Israel (1979), *Perception, Opportunity and Profit*, Chicago: University of Chicago Press.

Kirzner, Israel (1986), *Discovery and the Capitalist Process*, Chicago: University of Chicago Press.

Knight, F.H. (1921), *Risk, Uncertainty and Profit*, New York: Houghton Mifflin.

Knight, Russell M. (1983), "Entrepreneurship in Canada", *Journal of Small Business*, Canada, Vol. 1, No. 1, pp. 9–15.

Lindbeck, Assar (1973), "The Mainspring of Economic Growth", Nobel Memorial Lecture, 27 April 1973, in *Nobel Lectures Economic Science, 1969–80*, Singapore: World Scientific, pp. 135–46.

McMullan, W. Ed. and Wayne A. Long (1990), *Developing New Ventures*, San Diego: Harcourt Brace Jovanovich.

Marshall, A. (1961), *Principles of Economics*, 9th Edition, New York: Macmillan, first published 1890.

Maslow, A.H. (1954), *Motivation and Personality*, New York: Harper & Row.

Mugler, Josef (1990), "Entrepreneurship and the Theory of the Firm", in *New Findings and Perspectives in Entrepreneurship*, edited by Rik Donckels and A. Miettinen, Aldershot: Avebury, pp. 3–15.

Murayama, Motofusa (1982), "The Japanese Business Value System", in *Japanese Management, Cultural and Environmental Considerations*, edited by Sang Lee and Gary Schwendiman, New York: Praeger, pp. 89–116.

Okawara, Yoshio (1982), "Japan-United States Business Relationships", in *Japanese Management, Cultural and Environmental Considerations*, edited by Sang Lee and Gary Schwendiman, New York: Praeger, pp. 3–5.

Peters, Thomas J. and Robert H. Waterman, Jr (1982), *In Search of Excellence: Lessons from America's Best-Run Companies*, New York: Harper & Row.

Pleitner, Hans J. (1986), "Entrepreneurs and New Venture Creation: Some Reflections of a Conceptual Nature", *Journal of Small Business and Entrepreneurship*, Vol. 4, No. 1, pp. 34–43.

Schumpeter, J. (1934), *The Theory of Economic Development*, Boston: Harvard University Press, first published 1911.

Schumpeter, J. (1939), *Business Cycle*, Vol. 1, New York: Houghton Mifflin.

Seidler, Lee (1986), "Accounting Regulations in the US: The Growing Debate. Keynote Interviews by Professor Edward Stamp: The Analyst's View", in *Accounting Standards Overload*, edited by Raymond W.Y. Kao, Vancouver: Accounting Standard Authority of Canada, pp. 6–7.

Index

207

unemployment insurance, 111
uninformed optimism. *See* optimism
United States
    democracy. *See* democracy
    management practice, 55
    Stock Exchange Commission, 52

value(s). *See also* personal values
    adding, 84, 85, 95, 96, 106, 107,
        123, 126, 133, 135, 149, 158,
        165, 171, 174, 176
    creation, 87
    systems, 168
variable cost. *See* cost
venture
    capitalists, 122, 180
    creation, 177

start-up, 90, 179
voting in democracy vs in a firm,
    11–2
Vroom, Victor, 56

Waterman, Robert H., Jr, 24, 97,
    98, 128, 149
wealth, 8, 173
    creation, 84, 85, 87, 89, 90, 94,
        95, 96, 106, 107, 126, 133,
        135, 149, 158, 165, 171, 174,
        176
Wealth of Nations, 24
Weber, Max, 55, 56
wisdom, 99, 100, 122, 126, 134, 166,
    173
World War II, 7, 23, 101, 104, 140

About the Author

RAYMOND W. Y. KAO is Special Advisor to The Centre of Entrepreneurship and The School of Business, Centennial College, Canada. He was Professor of Entrepreneurship and Academic Director, Centre for Entrepreneurship, Faculty of Management, University of Toronto; and was Visiting Professor to Nanyang Technological University, Singapore. He is a member of the Editorial Board of *internationales gewerbeauchiv*, Switzerland, and Executive Editor of the *Journal of Small Business and Entrepreneurship*. His other positions include Member of Consultative Committee to the Minister of Small Business and Tourism, Government of Canada; Distinguished Professor of Entrepreneurial Studies, Ryerson Polytechnical University (formerly Institute); and Tasman Fellow, University of Canterbury, New Zealand. He is Wilford L. White Fellow of the International Council for Small Business, and President of the organization in 1986–87. He was also President of the International Council for Small Business, Canada, in 1980–84. His family business experiences include President and Co-owner, Oceacraft (retailing shops), Toronto (1963–70), Chairman and CEO, CIMA Manufacturing Company Ltd. (1983–87), and Director, Kam-Lung Industrial Ltd., S.A. Costa Rica (1970–present).

His publications include *Small Business Management* (3rd edition), *Entrepreneurship and Enterprise Development, Accounting Standards Overload: Big GAAP Versus Little GAAP*, and *Entrepreneurship and New Venture Management* (with Russell M. Knight).